AS/A-L[...] [...]ide

Series Editor: Marian Cox

Songs of Innocence and of Experience

William Blake

Philip Allan Updates
Market Place
Deddington
Oxfordshire
OX15 0SE
Tel: 01869 338652
Fax: 01869 337590
e-mail: sales@philipallan.co.uk
www.philipallan.co.uk

ISBN 0 86003 779 7

Printed by Raithby, Lawrence & Co Ltd, Leicester

Environmental information
The paper on which this title is printed is sourced from managed, sustainable forests.

Contents

Introduction

Aims of the guide

The purpose of this Student Text Guide to William Blake's *Songs of Innocence and of Experience* is to enable you to organise your thoughts and responses to the poems, to deepen your understanding of their key features and aspects, and to help you to address the particular requirements of examination questions in order to obtain the best possible grade. The 1990 Oxford University Press edition of the poems has been used throughout. To avoid confusion, poems with similar or identical titles are followed by (I) or (E) to indicate whether they are from *Songs of Innocence* or *Songs of Experience*.

It is assumed that you have read and studied the *Songs* already under the guidance of a teacher or lecturer. This is a revision guide, not an introduction, although some of its content serves the purpose of providing initial background. It can be read in its entirety in one sitting, or it can be dipped into and used as a reference guide to specific aspects of the poems.

The remainder of this Introduction outlines the Assessment Objectives, with a summary of the requirements of the various boards and their schemes of assessment; a revision scheme, which gives a suggested programme for using the material in the guide; and advice on writing examination essays.

The Text Guidance section examines the contexts in which the *Songs* were written, key aspects and analysis of the poems.

The final section, Questions and Answers, includes model essay plans, examination essay titles and sample essays.

Assessment Objectives

The Assessment Objectives (AOs) for A-Level English Literature are common to all boards:

AO1	communicate clearly the knowledge, understanding and insight appropriate to literary study, using appropriate terminology and accurate and coherent written expression
AO2i	respond with knowledge and understanding to literary texts of different types and periods
AO2ii	respond with knowledge and understanding to literary texts of different types and periods, exploring and commenting on relationships and comparisons between literary texts

AO3	show detailed understanding of the ways in which writers' choices of form, structure and language shape meanings
AO4	articulate independent opinions and judgements, informed by different interpretations of literary texts by other readers
AO5i	show understanding of the contexts in which literary texts are written and understood
AO5ii	show understanding of the contexts in which literary texts are written and understood and evaluate the significance of cultural, historical and other contextual influences on literary texts and study

This can be summarised as:

AO1	clarity of written communication
AO2	informed personal response in relation to time and genre (literary context)
AO3	the creative literary process (context of writing)
AO4	critical and interpretative response (context of reading)
AO5	evaluation of influences (cultural context)

It is essential that you pay close attention to the AOs and their weighting for the board for which you are entered: your teacher will be able to give you this information. Once you have identified the relevant AOs and the weightings, you must address them *directly* and *specifically*, in addition to showing your overall familiarity with and understanding of the text and demonstrating your ability to offer a clear, relevant and convincing argument.

The examiners are seeking above all else evidence of an *informed personal response* to the text. A revision guide such as this can help you to understand the text and to form your own opinions, but it cannot replace your own ideas and responses as an individual reader.

Revision advice

For the examined units it is possible that either brief or more extensive revision will be necessary because the original study of the text took place some time previously. It is therefore useful to know how to go about revising and which tried and tested methods are considered the most successful for literature exams at all levels, from GCSE to degree finals. Below is a guide on how not to do it — think of reasons why not in each case.

Don't:

- leave it until the last minute
- assume you remember the text well enough and don't need to revise at all
- spend hours designing a beautiful revision schedule
- revise more than one text at the same time
- think you don't need to revise because it is an open book exam
- decide in advance what you think the questions will be and revise only for those
- try to memorise particular essay plans
- reread texts randomly and aimlessly
- revise for longer than 2 hours in one sitting
- miss school lessons in order to work alone at home
- try to learn a whole ring-binder's worth of work
- rely on a study guide instead of the text

There are no short-cuts to effective exam revision; the only way to know a text well, and to know your way around it in an exam, is to have done the necessary studying. If you use the following method, in six easy stages, for both open and closed book revision, you will not only revisit and reassess all your previous work on the text in a manageable way but will be able to distil, organise and retain your knowledge. Don't try to do it all in one go: take regular breaks for refreshment and a change of scene.

(1) Between a month and a fortnight before the exam, depending on your schedule (a simple list of stages with dates displayed in your room, not a work of art), you will need to reread the text, this time taking stock of all the underlinings and marginal annotations as well. As you read, collect onto sheets of A4 the essential ideas and quotations as you come across them. The acts of selecting key material and recording it as notes are natural ways of stimulating thought and aiding memory.

(2) Reread the highlighted areas and marginal annotations in your critical extracts and background handouts, and add anything useful from them to your list of notes and quotations. Then reread your previous essays and the teacher's comments. As you look back through essays written earlier in the course, you should have the pleasant sensation of realising that your writing on the text has improved. You will also discover that much of your huge file of notes is redundant or repeated, and that you have changed your mind about some beliefs, so that the distillation process is not too daunting. Selecting what is important is the way to crystallise your knowledge and understanding.

(3) During the run-up to the exam you need to do lots of practice essay plans to help you identify any gaps in your knowledge and give you practice in planning in 5–8 minutes. Past paper titles for you to plan are provided in this guide, some of which can be done as full timed essays — and marked strictly according to exam criteria — which will show whether length and timing are problematic for you. If you have not seen a copy of a real exam paper before you take your first module, ask to see a past paper so that you are familiar with the layout and rubric.

(4) About a week before the exam, reduce your two or three sides of A4 notes to a double-sided postcard of very small, dense writing. Collect a group of key words by once again selecting and condensing, and use abbreviations for quotations (first and last word), and character and place names (initials). (For the comparison unit your postcard will need to refer to key points, themes and quotations in both texts relevant to the specific theme or genre topic.) The act of choosing and writing out the short quotations will help you to focus on the essential issues, and to recall them quickly in the exam. Make sure that your selection covers the main themes and includes examples of symbolism, style, comments on character, examples of irony, point of view or other significant aspects of the text. Previous class discussion and essay writing will have indicated which quotations are useful for almost any title; pick those which can serve more than one purpose, for instance those which reveal character and theme, and are also an example of language. In this way a minimum number of quotations can have maximum application.

(5) You now have in a compact, accessible form all the material for any possible essay title. You do not need to refer to your file of paperwork again, or even to the text. For the few days before the exam, you can read through your handy postcard whenever and wherever you get the opportunity. Each time you read it, which will only take a few minutes, you are reminding yourself of all the information you will be able to recall in the exam to adapt to the general title or to support an analysis of particular passages.

(6) A fresh, active mind works wonders, and information needs time to settle, so don't try to cram just before the exam. Relax the night before and get a good night's sleep. In this way you will be able to enter the exam room with all the confidence of a well-prepared candidate.

Writing examination essays

Essay content

One of the key skills you are being asked to demonstrate at A-level is the ability to select and tailor your knowledge of the text and its background to the question set in the exam paper. In order to reach the highest levels, you need to avoid 'pre-packaged' essays which lack focus, relevance and coherence, and which simply contain everything you know about the text. Be ruthless in rejecting irrelevant material after considering whether it can be made relevant by a change of emphasis. Aim to cover the whole question, not just part of it; your response needs to

demonstrate breadth and depth, covering the full range of text elements: character, event, theme and language. Only half a dozen approaches are possible for any set text, though they may be phrased in a variety of ways, and they are likely to refer to the key themes of the text. Preparation of the text therefore involves extensive discussion and practice at manipulating these core themes so that there should be no surprises in the exam. An apparently new angle is more likely to be something familiar presented in an unfamiliar way and you should not panic or reject the choice of question because you think you know nothing about it.

Exam titles are open-ended in the sense that there is not an obvious right answer, and you would therefore be unwise to give a dismissive, extreme or entirely one-sided response. The question would not have been set if the answer were not debatable. An ability and willingness to see both sides is an Assessment Objective and shows independence of judgement as a reader. Do not be afraid to explore the issues and do not try to tie the text into one neat interpretation. If there is ambiguity, it is likely to be deliberate on the part of the author and must be discussed; literary texts are complex and often paradoxical, and it would be a misreading of them to suggest that there is only one possible interpretation. You are not expected, however, to argue equally strongly or extensively for both sides of an argument, since personal opinion is an important factor. It is advisable to deal with the alternative view at the beginning of your response, and then construct your own view as the main part of the essay. This makes it less likely that you will appear to cancel out your own line of argument.

Choosing the right question

The first skill you must show when presented with the exam paper is the ability to choose the better, for you, of the two questions on your text where there is a choice. This is not to say you should always go for the same type of essay (whole-text or passage-based) and if the question is not one which you feel happy with for any reason, you should seriously consider the other, even if it is not the type you normally prefer. It is unlikely but possible that a question contains a word you are not sure about, in which case it would be safer to choose the other one.

Don't be tempted to choose a question because of its similarity to one you have already done. Freshness and thinking on the spot usually produce a better result than the attempted recall of a previous essay which may have received only a mediocre mark in the first place. The exam question is unlikely to have exactly the same focus and your response may seem 'off centre' as a result, as well as stale and perfunctory in expression.

Essay questions fall into the following categories: close section analysis and relation to whole text; characterisation; setting and atmosphere; structure and effectiveness; genre; language and style; themes and issues. Remember, however, that themes are relevant to all essays and that analysis, not just description, is always required. Once you have decided which exam question to attempt, follow the procedure below for whole-text and passage-based, open- and closed-book essays.

(1) Underline all the key words in the question and note how many parts the question has.

(2) Plan your answer, using aspects of the key words and parts of the question as sub-headings, in addition to themes. Aim for 10–12 ideas. Check that the Assessment Objectives are covered.

(3) Support your argument by selecting the best examples of characters, events, imagery and quotations to prove your points. Remove ideas for which you can find no evidence.

(4) Structure your answer by grouping and numbering your points in a logical progression. Identify the best general point to keep for the conclusion.

(5) Introduce your essay with a short paragraph setting the context and defining the key words in the question as broadly, but relevantly, as possible.

(6) Write the rest of the essay, following your structured plan but adding extra material if it occurs to you. Paragraph your writing and consider expression, especially sentence structure and vocabulary choices, as you write. Signal changes in the direction of your argument with paragraph openers such as 'Furthermore' and 'However'. Use plenty of short, integrated quotations and use the words of the text rather than your own where possible. Use technical terms appropriately, and write concisely and precisely, avoiding vagueness and ambiguity.

(7) Your conclusion should sound conclusive and make it clear that you have answered the question. It should be an overview of the question and the text, not a repetition or a summary of points already made.

(8) Cross out your plan with a neat, diagonal line.

(9) Check your essay for content, style, clarity and accuracy. With neat crossings-out, correct errors of fact, spelling, grammar and punctuation. Improve expression if possible, and remove any repetition and irrelevance. Add clarification and missing evidence, if necessary, using omission marks or asterisks. Even at this stage, good new material can be added.

There is no such thing as a perfect or model essay; flawed essays can gain full marks. There is always something more which could have been said, and examiners realise that students have limitations when writing under pressure in timed conditions. You are not penalised for what you didn't say in comparison to some idealised concept of the answer, but rewarded for the knowledge and understanding you

have shown. It is not as difficult as you may think to do well, provided that you are familiar with the text and have sufficient essay-writing experience. If you follow the above process and **underline**, **plan**, **support**, **structure**, **write** and **check**, you can't go far wrong.

Text Guidance

Biography

Schooling and early influences

William Blake was born at 28 Broad Street, Golden Square, in the Soho region of central London, on 28 November 1757. His father ran a successful hosiery business. From a young age Blake displayed an unusual and unruly nature, which led to his parents' decision to educate him at home instead of putting him through formal schooling. Throughout his life Blake was prone to violent outbursts of temper, which made him a notoriously unreliable and difficult colleague. Blake spent much of his childhood wandering around London and the surrounding area (London was then a considerably smaller city than it is now) and on one such trip to Peckham Rye he had a splendid vision of a tree full of angels.

Although he was not formally educated, Blake was highly motivated and intelligent; by the age of 13 he was already composing the poems that would become *Poetical Sketches* and reading, according to his own account, the works of John Milton and the book of Isaiah. He also showed considerable talent as an artist, and attended Mr Pars's drawing school in The Strand from the age of 10. Here Blake was taught to copy from plaster casts of ancient sculptures, an influence evident in his later work. Unable to afford the fees of placing his son with a leading painter, Blake's father apprenticed him to the engraver James Basire. One of Blake's training exercises under the tutelage of Basire was to make drawings of the tombs and monuments in Westminster Abbey. Frequently, in his enthusiasm for his work, Blake would climb on top of the monuments to gain a better view. This was a time of highly significant experience for Blake in more senses than one: first, it instilled in him a love of Gothic art which was to inspire the vision of both his visual and verbal art; and second, it provided him with one literally visionary experience — one day, while working on his drawings, Blake witnessed a visionary medieval procession through the precincts of the great abbey church.

Art, literature and printing

Blake's taste in art and letters was unfashionable, a reflection of his character, which was so frequently at odds with the world and the people around him. He rejected the works favoured by contemporaries such as Sir Joshua Reynolds, preferring instead the works of Dürer, Raphael and Michelangelo. In literature, he avoided the elaborate structures of eighteenth-century verse, taking Elizabethan poets as his models — Shakespeare, Jonson and Spenser in particular. He also drew on the works of antiquity, whether genuine, such as Percy's *Reliques of Ancient English Poetry*, or pastiche, such as Macpherson's *Ossian* or the forgeries of Thomas Chatterton. These influences point to Blake's urge to mythologise the world, an impulse which marked much of his mature work.

In 1779, at the age of 22, Blake was admitted to the Royal Academy, founded by its then president, Sir Joshua Reynolds. He supported himself by working as a journeyman engraver, producing illustrations for novels and catalogues by drawing life models, casts and corpses. Friction quickly arose between Blake and his teachers — especially Reynolds and George Michael Moser, who sought to discourage Blake's fondness for the 'old, hard, stiff and dry unfinished works' of Raphael and Michelangelo and demanded that he work with 'less extravagance and more simplicity'. The one teacher Blake found congenial and open to his ideas was James Barry, who produced a sequence of grand historical paintings.

In 1782, Blake married Catherine Boucher. They moved to a house in Green Street, near Leicester Square, where they worked together on the publication of *Poetical Sketches*, which came out in 1783. Following the death of his father in 1784, they moved to 27 Broad Street, setting up a print-selling business with James Parker. The partnership lasted only 3 years, ending because of problems exacerbated by Blake's fiery nature. In the same year Blake's favourite younger brother, Robert, died. Blake was later to claim that the spirit of Robert came to him in a vision, revealing the technique for combining images and poems on the same printing plate. Blake first attempted this method in 1788, and by 1789, when he published the *Songs of Innocence*, the technique had been perfected. Blake and Catherine worked on this as a team, producing the books by hand.

Productivity and decline

The years that followed were the most productive period of Blake's life. The Blakes moved to Lambeth, then still a village, and a new, more spacious house that facilitated their work. The poetry of this period, in the wake of the 1789 French Revolution, became more overtly political. *The French Revolution, The Gates of Paradise, The Marriage of Heaven and Hell, The Visions of the Daughters of Albion* and *America, a Prophecy* all date from the years 1791–93, and the *Songs of Experience* followed in 1794, along with *Europe, a Prophecy* and *The First Book of Urizen*. These works illustrate the epic propensities and intentions of Blake's poetry and demonstrate the importance of vision in his work.

After 1795, Blake's fortunes began to decline. Although the years 1795–1800 saw the production of a sequence of his greatest paintings (*Nebuchadnezzar, Newton* and *The House of Death*), he was to prove a notoriously unreliable workman for others, and failed on a series of commissions, alienating himself from all but the most dedicated of his friends. Among these was the poet William Hayley, who invited the Blakes to live near him in Felpham, outside Chichester; they moved there in 1800. By 1802, however, the irascible Blake had grown tired of what he came to see as the patronising commissions of his friends Hayley and Thomas Butts, and matters worsened still further when he found himself summoned on a charge of sedition after allegedly assaulting a soldier and making treasonous statements.

Although he was acquitted of these charges in 1804, Blake returned to live in London, never truly recovering from the experience.

Blake felt that in London he could somehow make a new start. Such hopes, however, proved ill-founded. Even when he did secure a potentially lucrative commission to illustrate and engrave Robert Blair's influential poem 'The Grave', Blake failed to please and took the perceived rejection very hard. He became increasingly cantankerous and withdrew into a solitary life with Catherine. He continued to work on his own illuminated books, however, producing *Milton* and *Jerusalem*; he considered the latter — a poem of war, peace and liberty focused on London — to be his finest work. A private exhibition of his work received little attention, except a set of vitriolic reviews, presenting the artist as 'an unfortunate lunatic whose personal inoffensiveness secures him from confinement.'

Revival and recognition

Strangely, Blake's final years saw something of a reversal in his fortunes. Turning 60, he found himself the object of the admiration of a set of young artists headed by John Linell who called themselves 'The Ancients'. At the end of his life Blake successfully completed a series of commissions, among them illustrations for *The Book of Job* and Dante's *Divine Comedy*. This new-found recognition brought great happiness to the elderly artist, as he found himself at the heart of creative life, admired and respected as 'The Interpreter' by his younger colleagues. He ended his days living contentedly in Fountain Court, off The Strand, a place where he may have passed unwittingly the young Charles Dickens, who at this time worked in a blacking factory nearby. He died at the age of 69 on 12 August 1827 and was buried in an unmarked grave in the dissenters' cemetery at Bunhill Fields, where a commemorative stone now stands.

Poet, painter and engraver

As well as being a poet, Blake was an artist and an engraver, and throughout his life he produced prolifically in all of these areas.

From 1789, Blake and his wife began a revolutionary new method of book production, printing a sequence of books which were a synthesis of visual images and words. The combination of text and illustrations was not a new concept, and Blake was regularly involved in the illustration of the works of other poets, but the combined production of illustration and text as part of one and the same process was a departure. Blake came to believe that the two media were inseparable in his art and experimented with various methods of combining them. An informed 'reading' of the illustrations that accompany the poems, as well as a wider consideration of his pictures and engravings, is essential to an understanding of his work.

Blake recounted how he was inspired to undertake this new method of printing

by a visitation in a dream from the spirit of his deceased and beloved younger brother, Robert. According to an account in the *Blake Records* (Bentley 1969):

> ...after deeply perplexing himself as to the mode of accomplishing the publication of his illustrated songs without their being subject to the expense of letter-press, his brother Robert stood before him in one of his visionary imaginations, and so decidedly directed him in the way in which he ought to proceed, that he immediately followed his advice.

Blake's biographer Peter Ackroyd (1995) describes the process:

> His first step was to cut out plates from a large sheet of copper, using a hammer and chisel, and to prepare the surface for his labours upon it. Then he made out a rough design with white or red chalk and, with that as his guide, he used a camel-hair brush to paint the words and images upon the plate with a mixture of salad oil and candle-grease. This mixture resisted the aqua fortis (of vinegar, salt armoniack, baysalt and vert de griz purchased from the local druggist), which bit into the surrounding plate for three or four hours — this was normally achieved in two stages, so Blake could check upon the progress of the operation. After that time the words and images stood up, and stood out, as part of one coherent design. There were technical complications that Blake, a very practical and intelligent craftsman, managed to overcome — the most important being that he wrote the words backwards with his quill, so that when the image was printed in reverse they would always be the correct way round. He used various instruments to lend variety to his designs — among them quills, brushes of various thickness, as well as his own stock of engraving tools. After the plate was 'bitten in', to a depth of approximately one-tenth of a millimetre, he used a conventional printer's ball of cloth to ink or black the plate with burnt walnut oil or burnt linseed oil; the plate was then gently printed on Whatman paper. Once the design had been produced Blake gave the paper a preliminary 'wash' with glue and water, before hand-painting the words and images with a 'size colour' or 'distemper' made out of water, colour pigment and carpenter's glue.

These pages would then be arranged into book form before binding. This has resulted in many different first editions of the works, in which the colouring and the order of the poems differ. Twenty-one copies of the *Songs of Innocence* are known to exist, as well as a further 27 combined copies of the *Songs of Innocence and of Experience*, but there are no individual versions of the *Songs of Experience*. It can be helpful to consider the different orders in which the *Songs* appear and to think about how this affects the reader's response.

Illuminated poems

Blake's main illuminated poems are as follows:

- *Songs of Innocence* (1789)
- *The Book of Thel* (1789)
- *Visions of the Daughters of Albion* (1793)
- *America, a Prophecy* (1793)
- *Songs of Innocence and of Experience* (1794)

- *The First Book of Urizen* (1794)
- *Europe, a Prophecy* (1794)
- *Song of Los* (1795)
- *Book of Ahania* (1795)
- *Book of Los* (1795)
- *Vala, or The Four Zoas* (1795–1804)
- *Milton* (1804–08)
- *Jerusalem* (1804–20)

Illustrations for the *Songs*

A fully illustrated version of the *Songs* is published in the Oxford Paperbacks series, and many of the images Blake drew are available on the internet. Two of the illustrations are reproduced below.

'Introduction' from the *Songs of Innocence*   'The Sick Rose' from the *Songs of Experience*

Paintings

Blake's most significant purely visual works are listed below. The location of the originals is also noted. It is well worth seeing these works full scale. Most of these images can be seen on the internet too.

- *Newton* (Tate Britain, London)
- *Nebuchadnezzar* (Tate Britain, London)

- *The Agony in the Garden* (Tate Britain, London)
- *The Body of Christ Borne to the Tomb* (Tate Britain, London)
- *The Raising of Lazarus* (Aberdeen Art Gallery)
- *The Ghost of a Flea* (Tate Britain, London)
- *The Body of Abel Found by Adam and Eve* (Tate Britain, London)
- *Satan Smiting Job with Sore Boils* (Tate Britain, London)
- *The Great Red Dragon and the Woman Clothed with the Sun* (Brooklyn Museum of Art)

Blake's London

By the end of the eighteenth century, London was the largest and probably the most diversely populated city in the world. From the extreme poverty of its eastern slums to the wealth of the aristocratic west, it was a city that provided a living for the whole spectrum of society. At the beginning of the eighteenth century it had a population of just under 600,000; by the year 1800, the city numbered over a million inhabitants, and by the time of Blake's death in 1827 it was well on its way to a mid-century count of over 2 million. The city was increasingly characterised by the youthfulness of its inhabitants, and there was a greater number of women than men. In the early years of the nineteenth century it also became an increasingly multi-cultural place: it had a significant number of Jewish, Chinese, Indian, eastern European, European and African inhabitants — all of which provided an interesting social background to a number of Blake's poems in the *Songs of Innocence and of Experience*.

This massive increase in population changed the topography of the city fundamentally. London originally comprised a series of communities hugging the Thames, each within easy reach of open fields, but by the turn of the nineteenth century it had become a massive urban sprawl. The once distinct communities merged into one another, encouraged by a programme of road and bridge building, and the city broke away from its narrow confinement along the banks of the river, making inroads into rural Middlesex and Surrey.

The new housing varied in quality, from the grand to the squalid. Until the London Building Act of 1774, which regulated building activities, house collapses were a frequent occurrence. This highlighted the already wide differences in social conditions that existed within the city. The slums of the East End and the north of the city expanded, fed by the increasing demand for labourers in the developing factories and the docks; they were characterised by poor infrastructure, poor housing and cramped, unhygienic conditions. In the meantime, the West End continued to develop as the wealthy heart of the metropolis. Formal squares were surrounded by the palaces of the aristocracy. The roads were well made, in contrast to the

mud-filled tracks of the rest of the city, and the streets were well lit. Water was supplied cleanly and efficiently, while elsewhere ground water had to be collected from unsanitary public wells. Clustering around these wealthy regions were back streets and mews houses, frequented by the artisans and tradesmen who served their rich neighbours, as well as by paupers and beggars.

Culturally and politically, the city was at the centre not only of the British Isles, but of the ever-widening British Empire. Its presses supplied news to the world, and its docks were busy with traffic to and from the rest of the known world. Coffeehouses, which were hotbeds of political, philosophical and literary thought, proliferated, as did theatres, and the metropolis became home to the vast majority of the great thinkers, authors, artists, scientists and medics of its day. Again, however, a marked contrast was evident. The liberal attitudes of coffeehouse society found no place on the streets and in the alehouses of the city, where religious bigotry, and anti-Catholicism in particular, was rife.

In the course of Blake's lifetime, therefore, the nature of the city of London changed almost beyond recognition. It developed from a compact, if densely populated, set of individual communities into the world's first great city, with all the positive and negative features such a change entails. In considering a poem such as 'London', the reader must be aware of the type of city Blake inhabited, a place of great diversity and vibrancy, but at the same time a place of extreme hardship for those not blessed with wealth. A number of the *Songs* deal with the relationship between the rural and the urban, which existed contiguously. The rural location of 'Introduction' (*Songs of Innocence*) was a nearby reality for eighteenth-century Londoners, providing a contrast to urban industrialism and squalor. However, the reader needs to remember that the distinction between the rural and the urban for Blake and his contemporary Londoners would not have been as dramatic as it is today.

Politics and revolution

Because his life spanned an era of such profound change it is impossible to separate Blake's works from the political and social climate within which they were produced. The American War of Independence took place in 1775 and the French Revolution in 1789, and at this time Britain was alive with political ferment and the consequent fear that the same events might be replicated at home. Furthermore, the industrial revolution was beginning to take hold and London, along with the northern industrial cities, was expanding rapidly, increasing political and social pressures.

Blake and politics

Blake was familiar from an early age with political radicalism, because he came from a dissenting religious background and an artisan family. During his youth, Blake

would have witnessed the continual changes — both political and social — in the city around him, where mob justice was a regular feature and where riots about religious issues and lack of food were not uncommon. He is known to have been present at the Gordon Riots of 1780, sparked by the Protestant Association, which opposed a parliamentary Bill seeking to lift some of the restrictions and penalties imposed on Roman Catholics. The riots culminated in the destruction of Newgate Prison, a scene depicted by Dickens in *Barnaby Rudge*.

The historian J. Paul De Castro describes how these riots left 'every man, woman and child in the streets panic struck, the atmosphere red as blood with the ascending fires'. Perhaps the fire and destruction on the streets of London and Paris account for some of the images in Blake's works. 'The Tiger', for example, is full of echoes of fiery apocalypse.

Blake and revolution

There is evidence to suggest that Blake was a committed revolutionary. At a time when it was dangerous to support events in France, it seems that Blake backed the French revolutionaries openly. Alexander Gilchrist, one of Blake's earliest biographers, wrote:

> Blake was himself an ardent member of the New School, a vehement republican and sympathiser with the Revolution, hater and contemner of kings and king-craft...he courageously donned the famous symbol of liberty and equality — the *bonnet rouge* — in open day, and philosophically walked the streets with the same on his head.
>
> (*The Life of William Blake*, p. 93)

Poems such as 'The Tiger' can be taken as an expression of revolutionary spirit. A further example is the following passage taken from the end of *The Marriage of Heaven and Hell*, a work produced at the same time as the *Songs of Innocence and of Experience*:

> The fire, the fire, is falling! Look up! Look up! O citizen of London, enlarge thy countenance...Spurning the clouds written with curses, stamps the stony law to dust, loosing the eternal horses from the dens of night, crying empire is no more! and now the lion and wolf shall cease.   (*The Marriage of Heaven and Hell*, Plates 25–27)

In 'The French Revolution', Blake offers his own unique portrayal of the events of 1789. The opening lines of the poem set the tone:

> The dead brood over Europe, the cloud and vision descends over cheerful France;
> O cloud well appointed! Sick, sick, the Prince on his couch, wreath'd in dim
> And appalling mist, his strong hand outstretch'd, from his shoulder down the bone
> Runs aching cold into the sceptre, too heavy for mortal grasp, No more
> To be swayed by visible hand, nor in cruelty bruise the mild flourishing mountains.
>
> (*The French Revolution*, ll. 1–5)

A passionate defender of liberty and the rights of expression, Blake suffered for his honesty. During a brief period of residence at Felpham on the Hampshire coast, he had a violent disagreement with a soldier billeted in the area and found himself under trial for sedition and the expression of anti-monarchical sentiments, and supposedly for expressing his support for Napoleon, with whom Britain was at war.

Blake and social reform

As well as addressing political and international issues, Blake was profoundly concerned with the concept of social justice. Like the French philosopher and novelist Jean Jacques Rousseau (see pp. 28–29), he believed in the need for social responsibility and for some form of social contract. Living in a city where a surge in population went hand in hand with extensive industrial development, Blake was outraged by the deep social divides and injustices he saw. Several of the poems in the *Songs of Innocence and of Experience* address these issues directly.

The 'Holy Thursday' poems in both sections of the text deal with the issue of charity. On the first Thursday in May as many as 6,000 children from London's charity schools were taken to a special church service at St Paul's Cathedral. This tradition dated from 1782, just a few years before the composition of the *Songs*, which suggests that the 'Holy Thursday' poems refer to these occasions. The *Songs of Innocence* version can be read in two ways — either as a straightforward depiction of childhood innocence, or as a deeply ironic critique of the social conditions that made the existence of charity schools a necessity. While nominally a good thing, charity actually appears to be an unholy, miserly and degrading dispensation from on high. Rather than extending freedom to the poor, it becomes yet another means by which they are ensnared within the system.

The poem can be compared with 'The Little Black Boy' and 'The Chimney-Sweeper', in which Blake uses the naive view of the child to portray the existence of more sinister realities. 'The Little Black Boy' is influenced by Britain's involvement in the slave trade and the dependence of the British economy upon the fruits of slave labour. In the course of Blake's lifetime, a radical shift in attitudes towards Britain's involvement in the slave trade and the role of slave labour came about. The formation of the Society for the Abolition of the Slave Trade in 1787 began a train of events that culminated in the eventual liberation of slaves in 1833.

Chimney-sweepers provide another target for Blake's social comment. Children were used to sweep chimneys because they were small enough to climb up over the flue; it was a dangerous job, exposing children to lung and eye diseases, and even suffocation. The two 'Chimney Sweeper' poems demonstrate the extent of Blake's anger at this situation. Like 'The Little Black Boy' and 'Holy Thursday', both poems show Blake's social awareness and powers of incisive criticism. The simplicity of the poems' form makes a bold statement.

Blake's views about organised religion are significant too. His dissenting background led him to view the power structures and legalism that surrounded religious establishments with distrust. He saw these as unwarranted controls over the freedom of the individual and contrary to the nature of a God of liberty. Poems such as 'The Garden of Love', 'The Little Vagabond', 'A Little Boy Lost' (E) and 'A Little Girl Lost' (E) make clear the extent of Blake's outrage at the impositions of the organised church on the individual.

Religion, morality and the Bible

Blake was a profoundly religious man, and is widely recognised as one of the foremost religious poets, alongside George Herbert, John Donne, John Milton and Gerard Manley Hopkins. His writings are full of biblical references and concepts with which readers need to be familiar.

Religion, myth and morality

Blake's religious views were highly idiosyncratic. He rejected many conventional beliefs and was outspoken about organised religious authority, which he viewed with suspicion. His beliefs about God and the relationship between God and mankind were influenced by the theologian Swedenborg (see pp. 29–31). However, Blake's engagement with the issue of religion was not just theoretical — it applied to the world around him too.

His criticism of restrictive conventional morality is apparent in poems such as 'A Little Girl Lost' (E) and 'The Garden of Love'. Contrary to the view that pleasure leads to corruption, Blake believed that it was the suppression of desire, not the enactment of it, that produced negative effects. This is seen throughout his works. Within his personal mythology, developed in his later poems, he uses characters such as Orc and Los to embody desires and their 'creative' energies and powers. In *The Marriage of Heaven and Hell* Blake expresses these ideas with compelling extremity: 'Sooner murder an infant in its cradle than nurse unacted desires' (Plate 10, 8). Blake not only couches his elevation of activity over passivity in provocative terms, but also pits himself against the supposed morality of his time. Inactivity was seen as a virtue, because it suggested martyrdom and Job-like acceptance of suffering, an attitude which Blake railed against. The energy of activity, even if seen as conventionally evil (Satan travelled in Genesis, meaning energy was equated with hell), was theoretically acceptable to him.

The logical extension of these views was for Blake to see those who enforced this type of passive 'morality' as figures of undesirable repression, the corrupters of

natural behaviour. Figures such as the schoolmaster in 'The Schoolboy', the parents in 'The Chimney-Sweeper' poems, the guardians of the poor in the 'Holy Thursday' poems, Ona's father in 'A Little Girl Lost' and the priestly representatives of organised religion in many of the poems, are for Blake the embodiment of evil restriction. Later he was to develop the mythological figures of Urizen and Tirzah as representations of repression; these both either appear or find their counterparts in the *Songs of Innocence and of Experience*.

Biblical language and imagery

The impact of the prophetic literature of the Bible on Blake's writings is profound, and can be seen in the stately language and the heavily prophetic tone of much of his output, including a number of poems within the *Songs*. The books of the Old Testament prophets, such as Psalms, Isaiah, Daniel, and the New Testament book of Revelation, all provide allusive sources for these poems, which import into the text a profound respect for the concepts of prophecy and vision.

Blake also frequently employs language that reflects the authoritative and deliberately weighty tone of the King James Bible. The possibility (indeed, the desirability) of creating multiplicity of meaning lay at the heart of the translators' business in creating the King James version, as Adam Nicolson points out (*Power and Glory* 2004, HarperCollins). Blake frequently uses such deliberate multiplicity in his writings.

The 'Little Girl' poems

The image of Lyca and her parents **wandering in the wilderness** links to the book of Exodus — following their release from slavery under Pharaoh in Egypt, the Israelites spent 40 years wandering in the wilderness. Jesus, too, spent 40 days in the wilderness following his baptism, where he was tempted by Satan (Luke 4). Many individuals in the *Songs* are wanderers, suffering from isolation and bewilderment.

Lyca is referred to as a **virgin**, which evokes Mary, the mother of Jesus. The image of the virgin is used repeatedly in the Bible to signify purity. In Revelation, the church is pictured as the virgin bride of Christ at the Second Coming. Virginal purity is frequently absent from the world of the *Songs*, however, where a far more problematic vision of innocence is offered.

The number **seven**, which is both Lyca's age and the number of days her parents search for her, is used repeatedly in the Bible. It is seen as a mystical number of completion — particularly in Revelation, where the images include seven churches, seals, bowls, plagues and trumpets.

The **lion** is a significant image: it occurs as a symbol of God's power when Jesus is referred to as the Lion of Judah (Revelation 5:5), but also has implications of threat, as in the story of Daniel in the lions' den (Daniel 6). The lion links to an array of wild beasts in the poems, but most significantly elicits comparison between the regal Christ and the frail and sacrificial lamb.

The image of a horde of **beasts** surrounding the vulnerable young Lyca calls to mind the vision of Isaiah, who foresees a time when beasts will live in peace, and predator and prey will lie down next to each other (see Isaiah 11:6–9). As threats to innocence, these beasts provide a physical externalisation of the more abstract threats within the text.

The lamb

The lamb is a central symbol within the Christian tradition, representing innocence and sacrifice. It is an animal that appears regularly in the *Songs* and deserves close attention. In the Bible, lambs are found in the following instances:

- Abraham refers to the lamb as a sacrificial animal (Genesis 22:8).
- Lambs have a ceremonial role in the Jewish feast of Passover, celebrating the sparing of the first-born sons of the Jews in the plagues of Egypt (Exodus 12).
- The lamb is a sign of salvation throughout the Old Testament, but comes to its full significance in the comparison of Jesus Christ to a lamb at the beginning of his earthly ministry, when John the Baptist calls him 'the lamb of God, who takes away the sin of the world!' (John 1:29).
- The train of lamb imagery comes to an extended climax in Revelation, where Christ is repeatedly referred to as the Lamb.

The shepherd

Linked closely with the image of the lamb, the shepherd is another central symbol in the Bible canon and in the *Songs*. 'The Shepherd' is the most obvious example of Blake's use of this image, but it is also significant in poems such as 'A Dream', the 'Little Girl' poems, 'The Voice of the Ancient Bard', the 'Little Boy' poems, 'London', and all those that include ideas of leading and misleading. There are a number of important ideas to remember:

- The figure of the shepherd represents protection. In the Old Testament, God is frequently referred to as the shepherd of the people of Israel.
- The Jewish King David began life as a shepherd boy before his defeat of the giant Goliath. His famous Psalm 23, which begins 'The Lord is my shepherd...', uses the imagery of shepherding.
- Shepherds were among the first to witness the birth of Christ at Bethlehem.
- Christ tells the famous parable of the Good Shepherd (John 10) to express his relationship with his followers.
- The image implies an intimate and knowing relationship between the shepherd and his sheep. The shepherd would gain the trust of his sheep by protecting them from predators (1 Samuel 17:34–36) and would walk with them, leading them to safety and new pastures.

A loving and caring God

The Bible repeatedly encourages the reader to see God as a parent figure, an idea of importance in poems such as 'A Dream', 'The Shepherd' and the 'Little Girl' poems. In a similar manner, 'On Another's Sorrow' presents God as a loving and paternal figure who cares for and tends his creation 'night and day'. The picture of God 'wiping all our tears away' calls to mind both Revelation 21:3–4 and Revelation 7:16–17. In the final three stanzas of the poem Blake emphasises God's desire to know his people and experience their life on earth. He does this by becoming 'an infant small', which suggests Christ's birth. (The illustrations of the *Songs*, particularly those for 'Infant Joy', evoke this too.) God's love for his people leads to suffering; when Blake refers to Christ as 'a man of woe', he recalls the words of the prophet Isaiah, who foresaw Christ's crucifixion and suffering.

This view of God contrasts sharply with that given in the *Songs of Experience*, where Blake presents a far harsher version of God, one who sometimes seems to be at war with his own creation. 'Introduction' (E), 'Earth's Answer' and 'A Poison Tree' may be interpreted as poems dealing with the enmity between God and humanity.

Wind and song

In 'Holy Thursday' (I), the difference between the hypocritical religion of the guardians of the poor and the genuine faith of the innocent children is underlined by Blake's use of two significant biblical images, both of which draw a picture of God's power. The 'mighty wind' recalls the story of the prophet Elijah on Mount Horeb, in which God's coming is preceded by 'a great and powerful wind [that] tore the mountains apart and shattered the rocks before the Lord' (1 Kings 19:11). It also bears a striking resemblance to a passage early in Acts, in which the coming of the Holy Spirit is preceded by 'a sound like the blowing of a violent wind' (Acts 2:2). We might infer that the 'mighty wind' of the poem will bring God's aid to the innocent children. The children's singing is described as 'harmonious thunderings', an oxymoron which alludes to the end of Revelation, in which John, approaching the climax of his vision of the new heaven, hears 'what sounded like the roar of a great multitude in heaven shouting' (Revelation 19:1). This suggests the heavenly nature of the children's innocent praise, and also great power.

Water

Water is an important image in the *Songs*, particularly in 'Night'. In the Bible, water, especially in the form of rivers, is a powerful symbol of rebirth and cleansing, as well as a provider of sustenance.

- The Israelites' passage through the Red Sea after their escape from Pharaoh can be seen as prefiguring the rite of baptism.
- The prophet Ezekiel has a vision of a holy river in Ezekiel 47:1–12. This anticipates the appearance of the river at the end of Revelation.

- Revelation makes extensive use of the image of the river flowing through the new Jerusalem (even though the earthly Jerusalem is not built on a river):

  > Then the angel showed me the river of the water of life, as clear as crystal, flowing from the throne of God and of the Lamb down the middle of the great street of the city. On each side of the river stood the tree of life, bearing twelve crops of fruit (Revelation 22:1–2).

- Jesus Christ is baptised by total immersion in the River Jordan by John the Baptist (John 3), an act which is taken to represent the death of the imperfect body and the resurrection of the new, perfect, spiritual body.

The connotations of the Thames in 'London' should be considered alongside the biblical use of water. The river may be a suggestion of hope and new life in the midst of the dark despair of the city, or it may be a Styx-like river of death, deliberately designed to contrast with biblical images of purity.

Trees

Trees are significant in a number of biblical passages, and Blake uses them to illustrate 'The Human Abstract', 'A Poison Tree', 'The Tiger', 'Introduction' (E) and 'Earth's Answer'. The image of the Tree of the Knowledge of Good and Evil from the Garden of Eden is key to understanding Blake's use of tree imagery within the *Songs*.

- See Genesis 2:8–9 and 15–17 for the Tree of Knowledge.
- In Mark 11:12–14 Christ curses a tree for its lack of fruit. This story is also included in Matthew 21:19, with the added detail that the tree instantly withers and dies.
- In Matthew 3:10, John the Baptist teaches using the image of a tree. Here the concept of good and bad fruit is introduced, which is a key idea in 'A Poison Tree'. Luke 3:9 also includes this story.
- Jesus uses the example of fruit trees to illustrate his teachings about true and false prophets in Matthew 7:15–20.

The word

The word is an essential concept in the New Testament: 'In the beginning was the Word, and the Word was with God, and the Word was God' (John 1:1) and impacts greatly on the world of the *Songs*. The subject is addressed explicitly in 'Introduction' (E). Words, whether of poetry or of prophecy, are linked integrally to the concept of God being the 'Holy Word'.

- Words have the power of creation. In Genesis, each phase of creation is prefaced by the words: 'And God said…' This implies that the word of God in itself has the power to call material from the void and to forge form from the formless.
- Words have the power to convey messages. Blake's poem opens with an injunction to 'Hear the voice of the bard!' Bards, or prophets, were frequently

called upon by God to pronounce messages of judgement and warning to his people. These are usually introduced with phrases such as 'Thus says the Lord' or 'The word of the Lord came to me, saying'.

■ The apostle John (John 1: 1–14) presents Christ as the synthesis of God's power and his message. Blake personifies the 'Holy Word' as that which 'walk'd among the ancient trees', a phrase reminiscent of the Genesis 3:8: 'And Adam and Eve heard the voice of the Lord God walking in the garden in the cool of the day.'

Words thus have great significance as the means by which God expresses himself, whether through creation, through the prophets, or in the form of Christ himself. In Blake's poem, however, it appears that the power of the word is ambiguous. The poem suggests that mankind rejects the voice of the bard, and thereby turns its back once more on God, whose distress at the loss of communication with his creation is suggested by the word 'weeping', and the direct appeal '"Why wilt thou turn away?"'

Love

Love, in its various manifestations, is one of the central concerns of the *Songs* (see pp. 83–84), and is dealt with specifically in 'The Clod and the Pebble'. Several quotations from the Bible provide an important background to this poem:

> Love must be sincere. (Romans 12:9).

> If I have not love, I am only a resounding gong. (1 Corinthians 13:1).

> Love is patient, love is kind. It does not envy, it does not boast, it is not proud. It is not rude, it is not self-seeking, it is not easily angered, it keeps no record of wrongs. Love does not delight in evil but rejoices with the truth. It always protects, always trusts, always hopes, always perseveres. (1 Corinthians 13:4–7).

Jesus and children

Poems such as 'The Lamb', 'The Divine Image' and 'A Cradle Song' draw on the connection between children and the baby Jesus, and this is particularly evident in 'The Chimney-Sweeper' (E). Jesus' teaching on the subject of children can be found in the following passages:

■ Matthew 19:13–14

■ Matthew 7:9–11

■ Matthew 18:5–6

■ Mark 9:36–37

Each of these passages emphasises the innocence and holiness of childhood. Causing children to sin, or deliberately leading them into the adult world of 'experience', constitutes an unnatural and sinful act.

Prohibition

In 'The Garden of Love', the gates of the chapel are shut to deter visitors and the chapel announces itself with the prohibition 'Thou shalt not'. This recalls two significant biblical passages:

- God gives the Ten Commandments to Moses on Mount Sinai in Exodus 20. Six of these begin with the formula 'Thou shalt not'.
- Deuteronomy 11:19–20 reinforces the need to drive home God's laws:

  Teach them to your children, talking about them when you sit at home and when you walk along the road, when you lie down and when you get up. Write them on the door-frames of your houses and on your gates.'

Human relations

The issue of human relations lies at the heart of the *Songs*. Blake deals extensively with the relationships between sectors of society and between individuals. There are two distinct biblical perspectives on this issue, contraries which inform many of the poems:

- Deuteronomy 19:21 states: 'Show no pity: life for life, eye for eye, tooth for tooth, hand for hand, foot for foot.' This is conventional revenge justice, an idea relevant to 'A Poison Tree'.
- The New Testament teachings of Christ are rather different. In Matthew 5:38–39 (responding directly to the passage from Deuteronomy) and Luke 6:27–28 he proposes treating enemies in a way that contrasts radically with Old Testament justice, instructing his followers to 'turn the other cheek'.

Visions, dreams and prophecies

Traditionally, visions were only vouchsafed by the worthy or innocent, such as saints, pious fasters, virgin maidens or imaginative children. Throughout his life, Blake was a firm believer in their importance and power. After Blake's death, his friend George Richmond kissed him and then closed his eyes 'to keep the vision in'. In the margin of Gilchrist's *Life of William Blake*, Richmond wrote:

> He said to me that all children saw 'visions' and the substance of what he added is that all men might see them but for worldliness or unbelief, which blinds the spiritual eye.

Blake appears to share this view with Milton — describing a visitation from Milton, he said:

> Of the faculty of Vision he spoke as One he had had from early infancy — He thinks all Men partake of it — but it is lost by not being cultivated. (Bentley, 1969)

Ackroyd, another of Blake's biographers, emphasises the importance of vision:

> In the visionary imagination of William Blake there is no birth and no death, no beginning and no end, only the perpetual pilgrimage within time towards eternity.

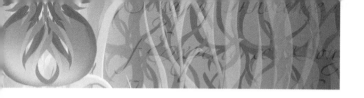

As a child Blake was once beaten by his mother for 'running in and saying that he saw the Prophet Ezekiel under a Tree in the Fields' (Bentley, 1969). Despite making a harsh impression on the young Blake, the experience apparently did not inhibit his visionary capacities. His life story is littered with accounts of visitations from spirits: the ghost of a flea; angels in the trees of Peckham Rye; the spirit in the sun; the departing spirit of his beloved brother Robert; even Satan himself. His paintings, engravings and poems are alive with his visionary imagination.

For Blake, vision involves more than ocular sight; it is, more importantly, an internal mechanism, by which physical reality is converted into personal spiritual development. The ability to 'see' is an integral part of the way in which humans reflect their divine creator; vision is the ability to move beyond the merely earth-bound into spiritual realms. It is for Blake an expression of the immortal and the eternal.

Fearful visions

Blake's visionary world is not a place of beatific and comfortable visions. Certainly these have their place, as do visions of inspiration, but frequently Blake's vision of the world is a fearsome one. His wife Catherine once observed: 'You know, dear, the first time you saw God was when You were four years old. And he put his Head to the window and set you ascreaming' (Bentley, 1969). The terrifying, reptilian ghost of a flea, according to Blake's own account, came at him with 'his eager tongue whisking out of his Mouth, a Cup in his Hands to hold Blood and covered with a scaly Skin of Gold and Green'. He also describes 'A Phantom…with Eyes like Coals, with long Teeth and Claws, scratching at us', a vision Blake goes on to identify as 'the Gothic fiend of our legends' — in other words, the devil. These examples testify to the profoundly disturbing nature of the visionary world Blake presents. Blake does not seek to comfort, but to present a vision of truth in all its various forms, a task that he saw as a divine gift. As he writes in *Milton*:

> For when Los joined with me he took me in his fiery whirlwind:
> My vegetated portion was hurried from Lambeth's shades,
> He set me down in Felpham's Vale and prepared a beautiful
> Cottage for me, that in three years I might write all these visions
> To display Nature's cruel holiness… (*Milton*, Book the Second, Plate 36, ll. 21–25)

This passage draws the reader's attention to the pervasive presence of contraries (see pp. 34–35) in Blake's vision. The juxtaposition of the city and the country, the bodily and the spiritual, cruelty and holiness, whirlwind and calm, encapsulate the mysterious nature of the vision Blake seeks to convey.

Prophecy

Blake's poetry is full of prophetic figures, and his language echoes the weighty utterances of biblical prophecies. The titles of a number of his books reflect this, particularly *Europe, a Prophecy* and *America, a Prophecy*. Other titles emphasise the visionary status of their contents, such as *The Visions of the Daughters of Albion*, or establish themselves alongside religious writings, for example *The Bible of Hell* and *Jerusalem*.

The *Songs of Innocence and of Experience* also frequently allude to and imitate the wisdom literature and prophecies of the Old and New Testaments. Blake uses a number of overtly prophetic figures, such as the Piper and the Ancient Bard, both of whom are established as more or less authoritative and apparently reliable. 'The Little Girl Lost' (I), for example, opens with the forceful and weighty claim:

> In futurity
> I prophetic see…

'A Little Girl Lost' (E) opens similarly, beginning with an appeal to the reader of the future in the clear anticipation of change:

> Children of a future age,
> Reading this indignant page,…

The *Songs* are full of characters who 'see', or at least strive to see, for example the searching emmet (an archaic name for an ant) of 'A Dream' and Lyca's parents in 'The Little Girl' poems. The limitations of their sight, however, are made clear — theirs is a blinkered vision, a world without foresight. They are unable to see beyond the confines of their current experience, which leaves them stranded in the present. Other 'seers' in the *Songs*, such as God in 'The Little Boy' poems and the speaker of 'On Another's Sorrow', display a greater clarity of vision.

Social change

The concept of vision in the *Songs* is often linked to social change. In presenting the world around him, Blake was always intensely alive to the possibilities or probabilities of the future and, in many cases, of the need to effect change. The opening lines of 'A Little Girl Lost' envisage a future where different attitudes to 'sweet love' may prevail. Such visionary insights and intentions become very clear in poems such as 'The Little Vagabond' and 'The Little Black Boy', in which children look forward to an ideal future of comfort and equality. In these poems, Blake confronts perceived social injustices and moral corruption, offering his reader a new vision of the future. It is perhaps a sign of Blake's visionary power and sense of social justice that he foresaw what later came to pass: after his death both chimney-sweeping by children and slavery were abolished.

Dreams and revelations

In Blake's poetry, dreams are not simply expressions of a subconscious fantasy world, but carry significant meaning. Among others, the dreams of the emmet in 'A

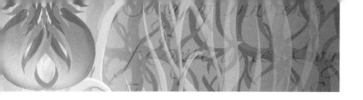

Dream' and Tom Dacre in 'The Chimney-Sweeper' (I) can be seen as forms of spiritual revelation. It is significant that dreams are often the medium by which Old Testament prophets receive their visions; as the prophet Joel writes:

> I will pour out my spirit on all people. Your sons and daughters will prophesy, your old men will dream dreams, your young men will see visions. Even on my servants, both men and women, I will pour out my spirit in those days. (Joel 2:28–29)

Other poems are visionary in another sense. In 'The Divine Image' (I), 'The Human Abstract' and 'A Divine Image' (E), for example, Blake offers a sequence of visions of humanity and God as creator. Similarly, in 'The Tiger' and 'The Lamb' Blake presents two contrasting visions of the creator God. 'The Tiger' also arguably offers a vision of the potential threat of revolution.

Blake, Rousseau and Swedenborg

Two of the most important influences on Blake's views about life and religion were the French philosopher Jean Jacques Rousseau (1712–78) and the Swedish theologian and philosopher Emanuel Swedenborg (1688–1772).

Blake and Rousseau

The author of books such as *The Social Contract* and *Émile* (both 1762), Rousseau was an influential figure, especially in the revolutionary powder keg that was late-eighteenth-century Europe. His ideas inevitably influenced Blake's thoughts and works, but Blake's association with Rousseau's writings is by no means straightforward. A fervently religious man, Blake was deeply scornful of Rousseau's rejection of religious belief. He composed the following verses to express the strength of his feelings:

> Mock on, mock on, Voltaire, Rousseau:
> Mock on, mock on; 'tis all in vain!
> You throw the sand against the wind,
> And the wind blows it back again.
>
> And every sand becomes a gem
> Reflected in the beams divine;
> Blown back they blind the mocking eye,
> But still in Israel's path they shine.
>
> The atoms of Democritus
> And Newton's particles of light
> Are sands upon the Red Sea shore,
> Where Israel's tents do shine so bright.

However, there are subtle connections that can be drawn between the two writers' works. One of Rousseau's main concerns was that contemporary society, a place of growing industrial efficiency and production, was increasingly separating mankind from nature, and that this caused increasing unhappiness and loss of virtue. This is significant when considering *Songs of Innocence and of Experience*, because Blake repeatedly presents the reader with a similar set of contraries, exploring questions of innocence vs experience and virtue vs vice within a range of contexts.

Furthermore, Rousseau believed that society imposed restraints on individuals, forcing them to comply with social expectations and to bury their individuality. This, he felt, would lead to the suppression of people's true emotions and a consequent sense of alienation from the rest of mankind. These ideas link directly to the philosophical and psychological world of the *Songs,* in images such as the 'mind-forged manacles' of 'London', or the plight of the chimney-sweeper, the nurse or the little black boy.

Rousseau thought that the solution to these social problems was to recognise the rights of the individual, and of the under-privileged individual in particular. He assumed that people have an innate sense of justice and virtue which leads to principled action, and believed in the need for a new philosophy of education. The removal of adult restrictions and impositions would leave the child free to learn by experience. This, Rousseau believed, would lead to the formation of a popular social contract under which everyone could flourish. Again, the connection of these ideas to Blake's *Songs* is evident. Poems such as 'The Schoolboy', 'A Little Boy Lost', 'A Little Girl Lost' and others deal directly with these issues, and it is clear that Blake was a fervent advocate of the need for social equality and justice (see pp. 18–19). 'The Human Abstract' is also significant in this context, because it explores the obstructions to the existence of a social contract.

Blake and Swedenborg

Blake's links with the teachings of the Swedish scientist and theologian Emanuel Swedenborg are complex. Swedenborg never established a church himself, but his followers set up the New Jerusalem Church, based on his teachings. Blake first became involved with Swedenborg's teachings in 1787, when he began to study and annotate his works. Blake and his wife attended a general conference at the Swedenborgian Chapel in Great East Cheap in 1789, the year in which *Songs of Innocence* was published. Blake's writings are profoundly influenced by Swedenborg's philosophy, particularly the sequence of works dating between 1789 and 1793, comprising the *Songs of Innocence, The Marriage of Heaven and Hell* and the *Songs of Experience.*

Swedenborg did not accept the conventional Christian doctrine of the Holy Trinity, in which God is divided into three manifestations or states: the Father (the

omnipotent creator and sustainer of life); the Son (God's earthly manifestation as Jesus Christ); and the Holy Spirit (the presence of God in the world as a guiding spirit and inspiration). He argued instead for a unified vision of Jesus Christ, the 'divine human', as God.

Blake's poem 'The Divine Image' (I) builds on this idea, pursuing it to the conclusion that God is found in every human. The title can be taken to mean a poem presenting the poet's image of God, or a poem representing man created in God's image. Both are key ideas in the *Songs*, in which Blake explores mankind's relationship with and reflection of the divine. The dual nature of humanity is at the very heart of Blake's view of the world — humans sometimes display traits of godly perfection, but also frequently fail to live up to the divine image. This dichotomy is explored throughout the *Songs*, but is most specifically outlined in 'The Divine Image' (I) and its partner poem from *Songs of Experience*, 'The Human Abstract'.

Blake's thoughts about Christ, God in human form, are equally complex. In 'The Divine Image' (I), 'The Human Abstract' and 'A Divine Image' (E) Blake addresses these ideas directly; poems such as 'The Lamb', 'Infant Joy' and 'On Another's Sorrow' do so more subtly. Traditional theology, based on the Gospels, sees Christ as a figure who is simultaneously fully man and fully God, a meeting of the human and the divine. Milton encapsulates this idea in *Paradise Lost*, when he speaks of the 'human face divine' (*Paradise Lost* 3, line 44). Blake, however, adapts and develops Swedenborg's notion of a unified man and God in which God is to be found within every person. This idea is approached in 'The Lamb':

> He is callèd by thy name,
> For he calls himself a lamb.
> He is meek and he is mild;
> He became a little child.
> I a child and thou a lamb,
> We are callèd by his name.

Blake gave a more explicit, and yet more concise, expression of this belief in the following couplet from *The Everlasting Gospel*, where God says to Jesus:

> Thou art a Man; God is no more;
> Thy own humanity learn to adore. (Section C, 4.21–22)

It is vital to grasp the full implications of the difference between the conventional interpretation and Blake's view of the relationship between God and mankind. Blake does not claim, as the phrase 'God is no more' might seem to suggest, that God has ceased to exist. His meaning is that, from the point of Christ's birth onwards, God's highest representation takes the form of the divine man.

Swedenborg's influence can also be seen in Blake's interpretation of the Fall of humanity from the Garden of Eden. This is evidently an important subject for Blake, since it recurs throughout the *Songs*. Swedenborg did not view the event and its aftermath as the punishment of humanity by a just and regretful God, but rather as an act of vengeance by a 'Selfish father of men', as Blake puts it in 'Earth's Answer'. The poem explores Swedenborg's view that the banishment of Adam and Eve was a result of God's desire to limit the freedom of his creation. 'Introduction' and 'Earth's Answer' at the beginning of the *Songs of Experience* focus on this idea, and it is illuminating to read 'A Poison Tree' in this context. Freedom and restriction are clearly key concepts within Blake's view of the world and of the human condition.

To appreciate fully Blake's interaction with Swedenborg's ideas, it is helpful to consider *The Marriage of Heaven and Hell*, written and produced between the publication of the *Songs of Innocence* in 1789 and the first combined *Songs* in 1793. Pleasure and the act of love, Swedenborg suggests, are not characteristics of fallen human nature but signs of positive humanity. Blake observes in *The Marriage of Heaven and Hell* that: 'The soul of sweet delight can never be defiled' (Plate 9, 14). This view is relevant when applied to 'The Little Girl' poems, 'The Sick Rose' and 'The Blossom', which explore issues of sexual love, and 'The Schoolboy' and 'The Little Vagabond', both of which explore pleasure and comparative attitudes towards it.

A final example of Swedenborg's influence on Blake is the concept of correspondence. This is the belief that the physical object is only the visible part of a greater spiritual entity. Thus Blake concludes: 'Man has no body distinct from his soul; for that called body is a portion of soul discerned by the five senses, the chief inlets of soul in this age' (Plate 4). If this is true, it may go some way towards explaining the visionary capacity of Blake himself.

Milton and *Paradise Lost*

Milton's influence on Blake's writings, paintings and engravings is profound, since throughout his life Blake returned to the great poet for inspiration. As well as an appreciation for the past, Blake and Milton shared a religious fervour, although there were significant differences between their religious views — Blake believed that Milton was blinkered by his narrowly Protestant interpretation of the Bible. In addition, both men shared the faculty of experiencing visions, and it seems that Milton appeared to Blake on many occasions.

Blake produced illustrations for a range of Milton's writings. He chose scenes from *History of Britain* for his early historical paintings, and *Paradise Lost, Il Penseroso, L'Allegro*, and *On the Morning of Christ's Nativity* all provided inspiration for him. In addition, he produced a painting of Milton for the library of Turret House, the Hampshire home of his friend and patron, the poet William Hayley, and in 1810 wrote a long poem entitled *Milton* as a form of homage.

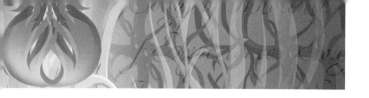

The cadences and formal properties of Milton's verse were powerful influences on Blake. Milton's prophetic approach must have appealed to the young poet, himself fired by visionary experiences. Blake sought to reproduce such epic dimensions in his own verse; his later poems, in particular, are marked by vast, Gothic canvases similar to those of *Paradise Lost*. But the smaller-scale poems of the *Songs of Innocence and of Experience* reveal Milton's influence, too — the prophetic fervour of many of the lyrics and the spiritual contraries they present fit into Milton's world. The conflict between good and evil, innocence and experience is at the heart of both authors' works, providing a vital and driving energy. Indeed, Blake believed that this conflict manifested itself in the creative process of Milton's most famous work, *Paradise Lost*; this view was made clear in this famous quotation from *The Marriage of Heaven and Hell*:

> Note. The reason Milton wrote in fetters when he wrote of Angels & God, and at liberty when of Devils & Hell, is because he was a true Poet and of the Devil's party without knowing it.

Milton's epic poem, *Paradise Lost*, first published in 1667, tells the biblical story of the temptation and Fall of humanity, as recorded in Genesis. Not only did Blake produce a series of illustrations for the poem, he also dealt with the same story and the issue of God's relationship with his human creation in the *Songs*. *Paradise Lost* tells of how Adam and Eve were created and, through an act of disobedience to God (eating the forbidden fruit), find themselves banished from the Garden of Eden. Milton also relates the story of Satan, originally known as Lucifer, an angel who leads an attempted rebellion against God, and who is punished by being sent to hell. His revenge is to cause the Fall of mankind by tempting Eve in the form of the serpent.

Milton's influence can also be found in a number of specific references within the *Songs*. In 'Introduction' (E) (explored fully on pp. 56–57) we are forced to question whether it is the bard, God or mankind 'That might control/ The starry pole/ And fallen, fallen light renew'. The starry pole seems to be an image of hope, a source of good to come in the future. This impression is strengthened if the allusion to *Paradise Lost* is appreciated; Milton uses the words 'starry pole' to describe the night sky watched by Adam and Eve prior to their fall. Thus the image seems to represent the possibility of a restoration of paradisal innocence for man and the earth.

The word 'pole' appears again in 'A Poison Tree', but this time it is 'veiled', indicating the extent to which man is separated from the divine. The poem also alludes to the fall from paradise, suggesting that the 'foe outstretched beneath the tree' has not suffered a literal death. For a more detailed analysis, see pp. 72–73.

Gothic and Romantic influences

The Gothic

From his earliest years, Blake was fascinated by the Gothic. As an apprentice to the engraver James Basire, he was sent to work in Westminster Abbey, where he immersed himself in the medieval Gothic architecture and spent hours drawing the tombs. His art and poetry, particularly the later epics, demonstrate a love of the bizarre and almost a sense of glee in excess and horror.

Grotesque and horrific images can be found in many late-eighteenth-century literary works by Edward Young, Robert Blair, Thomas Parnell and Thomas Gray. At the same time, the Gothic novel was emerging as a literary form in its own right, with novels such as *The Castle of Otranto* (1764) by Horace Walpole, *The Old English Baron* (1778) by Clara Reeves and William Beckford's oriental fantasy *Vathek* (1786). Blake was familiar with Gothic fiction, and some lines from Ann Radcliffe's *The Mysteries of Udolpho* (1794) are copied in his hand on the back of one of his prints. One of the few surviving paintings by his wife Catherine, a depiction of Agnes from Matthew Lewis's novel *The Monk* (1796), also betrays the influence of Gothic fiction.

Typical aspects of the Gothic

Many see the Gothic as a loosely defined form, but it is possible to identify various features that are typical of works falling within the genre. These are identified below, together with examples from Blake's poems:

- **Wild landscapes** — these can be seen in: the 'valleys wild' of the 'Introduction' (I); the 'wat'ry shore' of 'Earth's Answer'; the wildernesses of 'The Little Girl' and 'The Little Boy' poems; the 'forests of the night' in 'The Tiger'.
- **Ruined or grotesque buildings** — wild castles and other buildings are found in many of Blake's longer poems; 'London' is full of grotesque and oppressive buildings.
- **Religious settings and concepts** — churches and abbeys play an important part, often as symbols of oppression, as in 'The Garden of Love'; Blake's work reflects his own religious views (see pp. 19–25 and 29–31).
- **The supernatural and ghostly** — this is seen in the presence of angels in poems like 'The Angel', 'Introduction' (I) and 'The Chimney-Sweeper' (I) and the ghostly figure of the father in 'The Little Boy Lost'.
- **Imagery of darkness, shadow, decay** — examples include the dark world of 'Introduction' (E); the blackness of 'A Poison Tree' and 'The Human Abstract'; the dark streets of 'London'; 'The Tiger' with its 'forests of the night'.
- **The exotic and oriental** — elements of oriental fantasy litter the longer poems; exotic beasts, such as lions and tigers, are used.

- **Horror and terror** — 'London' offers a vision of a city of horrific possibilities; 'The Tiger' points to potential terror; 'A Poison Tree' explores the horror of inhumanity.
- **Isolation and loneliness** — this relates to both setting and characters, including orphans and widows; Blake often emphasises the isolation of his characters, even when they are surrounded by potential companions; although it teems with characters, 'London' is a dark and lonely place; Ona, Lyca and 'The Little Black Boy' all suffer isolation.
- **Blurring of distinctions between sanity and insanity** — this is seen in the pathological wrath of 'A Poison Tree'.
- **Sex and sexuality** — this includes the sexual overtones of the frequently used towers (phallus) and caverns (vagina); this is seen in the 'Little Girl' poems. A number of the *Songs* deal with the issues of sexual experience and threat; this is seen in 'The Sick Rose', 'The Blossom', 'The Angel' and 'My Pretty Rose Tree'.
- **Use of multiple narrators** — Blake uses a range of narrative voices throughout the collection; consider the different voices of the piper, the bard, the black boy and the chimney-sweepers.
- **Crime, lawlessness, abuse and absolute power** — these occur regularly, such as in the dangerous, lawless streets of 'London', and the suffering of the sweeps; Blake portrays various tyrannical power-figures, including those seeking to abuse, e.g. God in 'Introduction' (E) and 'Earth's Answer', Tirzah in 'To Tirzah', the father in 'A Little Girl Lost'.
- **Stock characters** — the absent mother (the 'Little Boy' poems), wicked father/father-figure ('A Little Girl Lost'), helpless heroine (the 'Little Girl' poems), the villain (often linked to religion) (numerous priests), hopeless lover ('The Angel'), and the outsider can all be found.
- **The devilish and arcane** — Blake recognises the presence and power of such forces; see books such as *The Bible of Hell*.
- **Use of the historical past** — Blake's work largely exists within the present, but has a timeless quality, at times reaching back into the ancient past, as in 'Earth's Answer'; Blake frequently seeks to place human experience within a historical/biblical context.

Blake, the Gothic and contraries

The frequent and significant presence of contraries in Blake's writings links him closely to the Gothic. It is a form that thrives on the recognition of opposition and division, investigating in detail the impact of (often unwholesome) 'experience' upon 'innocence'. Blake's use of contraries, however, is more subtle than in much Gothic writing, where dualism tends to take the form of stark opposition.

The importance of contraries to his work can be seen in the titles of his two collections: *Songs of Innocence* and *Songs of Experience*. The subtitle *Shewing Two*

Contrary States of the Human Soul points to this too. In *The Marriage of Heaven and Hell* (another title which foregrounds the notion of contraries), Blake writes: 'Without contraries is no progression. Attraction and repulsion, reason and energy, love and hate, are necessary to human existence.' Blake does not deal in simple opposites, qualities that oppose and negate each other; the contraries he identifies often create uncertainty and are frequently the cause of discomfort, but they are always a source of vital energy. The creative process and life itself spring from the constructive presence of contraries within human nature.

Below is a list of the most commonly used contraries and divisions within Blake's writings. Look for these contraries as you read the poems and consider in detail how they affect the response of the reader. The list is not intended to be exhaustive, so add any others you discover as you read.

- innocence and experience
- day and night
- light and dark
- good and evil
- freedom and constraint
- the permissible and the forbidden
- truth and deception
- kindness and harshness
- summer and winter
- life and death
- the transient and the eternal
- the finite and the infinite

- God and humanity
- child and adult
- ascent and descent
- creativity and reason
- soul and body
- the spiritual and the sensual
- salvation and damnation
- natural and unnatural
- blessing and curse
- perfection and corruption
- wealth and poverty
- God and Satan

Romanticism

The Romantic period (roughly 1775–1840) influenced subsequent literature profoundly. Romanticism's chief tenets are the importance of childhood, passion, the individual, the personal, love and nature. Romantic texts remind us of the fairy-tale tradition we have been familiar with since bedtime stories. According to this approach to life, feelings are to be trusted rather than thoughts, and impulses followed are safer than rules obeyed. Romantics champion rebellion, non-conformity and the cause of the little man against the system. They prefer to be outdoors and revere nature as a divine force; those who cut themselves off from their natural roots in the countryside will perish spiritually. Romantics believe that not everything can or should be explained by logic or science, and that some mystery should be left in the world because the creative human imagination needs to feed on magic and fantasy. Because everything is in a state of flux — and therefore happiness, youth, beauty, innocence and emotions are ephemeral — it is necessary to *carpe diem* (seize the day) and spontaneously snatch fleeting pleasure from the

jaws of time. Because of the inevitability of loss, pain, physical decay and old age, the Romantic mode is a tragic one, often involving someone dying young.

There were significant political and intellectual developments in this period. Rousseau's *The Social Contract* asserted the rights of the individual and the need for greater social responsibility, while in England essayists such as Thomas Carlyle and William Godwin formed a new political agenda. Political thought led to a powerful sense of national rights and national identity, and questioned the legitimacy of the concepts of monarchy and aristocracy, culminating in revolutions in France and America.

The uncertainty, unrest and excitement of the Romantic period is reflected in its music, visual arts and writing. As the power of the old aristocracy diminished, the role of patronage also declined, affecting artists in a variety of ways. Some, such as Sir Walter Scott, Lord Byron and Percy Bysshe Shelley, were freed to carve their own niche in the new literary marketplace, while others, including Blake, were left to plough their own lonely furrows of artistic exploration. These developments led to the stereotype of the Romantic artist as a hermit-like and prophetic figure, somehow divorced from social conventions and the everyday hierarchy.

Romanticism can be seen as a reaction against the rationalism of the Enlightenment that preceded it. In the face of what they perceived as cold empiricism (i.e. assessing the world on the basis of experience and fact), the Romantics asserted the importance of individual feeling. Wordsworth warned against the 'meddling intellect' and looked for a return to the sanctuary of the human heart. He argued that science was the negation of poetry, a view that Blake seems to share. Many of the Romantics elevated nature, seeing in it a reflection of the soul, the sublime and the divine.

Blake was not merely influenced by Romanticism; he was its forerunner, and elements of the cultural development he heralded can be traced in his work and his personality. Profoundly individual in his approaches both to life and to the creation of his works of art, a social misfit frequently at odds with those around him and deeply suspicious of organised authority, he can be seen as an archetypal Romantic figure. The following sections outline some of the key links between Blake and the Romantic movement.

Visions

The Romantics placed great importance on the visionary and the prophetic, which were seen as bringing humans in touch with divine revelation. Blake's poems contain strong elements of visions and prophecy, and this is suggested by the titles of his main works, for instance *The Marriage of Heaven and Hell* and *Visions of the Daughters of Albion*. The *Songs of Innocence and of Experience* are presented as a visionary exploration of the contrary states of human nature and its manifestations. The importance of visions in Blake's poetry is explored in more detail on pp. 25–28.

Revolution

In keeping with the mood of the times, Blake uses the theme of revolution repeatedly. *Europe, a Prophecy* and *America, a Prophecy* both deal with political revolution. The *Songs* also address such issues; the Earth in 'Earth's Answer' revolts against God's judgement, while other poems, such as 'The Little Black Boy' and both 'The Chimney-Sweeper' poems challenge contemporary conventions and beliefs. Blake and the Romantics overturned the contemporary idea that one should obey the head and not the heart. (For more detail on Blake and revolution, see pp. 17–18.)

Children

Like Rousseau and Wordsworth, Blake prioritises the view of children, seeing in their state of existence a model to emulate. (See pp. 28–29 for a fuller consideration of Blake's links with Rousseau.) Blake's presentation of children is complex, however. At times they appear innocent (as in 'Infant Joy') or naive (as in 'The Chimney-Sweeper' (I) or 'The Black Boy'), while elsewhere they take on a more sinister role ('Infant Sorrow' and 'London'). In the Augustan period (approximately 1700–45), children (and women and animals) had been thought unfit subjects for poetry.

Anti-rationalism

Blake was profoundly at odds with the rationalism of his age. This is apparent in his painting *Newton* (a man whom Blake despised), in which the scientist, engrossed in his work, remains oblivious to the marvellous manifestations of the sublime and the divine in the undersea world that surrounds him. For Blake, Newton embodied 'cold reason', a negative force often attacked in his poetry. These ideas inform the characterisation of Ona's father in 'A Little Girl Lost' and the priest in 'A Little Boy Lost'.

The mythological past

Blake developed his own mythological system (see pp. 76–79), far removed from the classical mythologies of Rome and Greece, although these have an influence on his poetry. Blake's mythological world appears to be a place of primitivism, for instance in the allusion to druids and pagan practices in 'Earth's Answer' and in his attempts to re-create the mythical Albion, which is seen to some extent in 'Introduction' (E).

Analysis of the poems

Songs of Innocence

'Introduction'

This poem (see Blake's illustrations on p. 14) provides an insight into the process of poetic composition. It introduces the piper, who may be a poetic persona or may be Blake himself. In either case, the piper is both the composer and the singer of the *Songs* that are to follow. Rambling through the 'valleys wild', the piper encounters a child. The figure might represent a cherub or an angel (Blake claimed, as a child, to have met with an angel while out playing on Peckham Rye, in south London), who acts as an inspiration for the creative process. Note how the poem begins with the piper already engaged in artistic activity, playing his tunes of 'pleasant glee' — songs without words. In stanza two, this develops into a song *with* words. The subject is the lamb, one of the key images of the collection; it is important not only as a symbol of youthful, carefree innocence, but also as one of the most powerful biblical images of Christ, who is presented as a sacrificial lamb. The piper is instructed to write down his songs in stanza four, and he begins the writing process that is completed in stanza five, when he creates his pen and ink from the natural materials that surround him. The movement from unformed music to fully formed poems is reflected in the transformation of the pipe into a pen.

The child's instructions to the piper are very clear and offer the reader a manifesto of Blake's intentions:

> 'Piper sit thee down and write
> In a book that all may read —'

This suggests that Blake's purpose in composing the *Songs of Innocence and of Experience* is twofold:

- to write a collection of poems that are universal in their significance
- to write poems that are simple in form and expression so that they may be read and understood by all

The rustic simplicity of this poem, set as it is in the 'valleys wild' near a babbling brook, prepares the reader to expect rural and idyllic subject matter. The rural setting seems pleasant and unthreatening (compare 'The Echoing Green' and 'Nurse's Song' (I)). However, in other poems the natural world adopts an altogether more sinister guise, as in 'The Little Girl Lost' and 'The Little Girl Found'. In 'Introduction' (I), words such as 'wild' and 'stained', along with the image of the lamb and its Christian overtones of sacrifice and suffering, may also suggest other, less ideal possibilities.

'A Dream'

This poem moves into the realm of dreams and visions, and introduces the concept of prophecy, which is continued at the opening of 'The Little Girl Lost' (I). This shift brings with it a darker and more threatening tone, which was only hinted at in 'Introduction' (I). The dream is described as a 'shade', an image laden with dark possibilities, and Blake's choice of vocabulary emphasises this, for example, 'Dark, benighted, travel-worn' and 'watchman of the night'. These images make the reader aware of the presence of forces which may overcome the innocence, goodness and happiness of the opening poem. The emmet (ant) finds herself trapped in the confusion of 'many a tangled spray', which reflects both her physical and psychological state.

Like the 'Little Girl' poems, 'The Chimney-Sweeper' and 'The Schoolboy', this poem deals with the separation of parents and children, which poses a fairy-tale threat to innocence. Tears make an appearance in this poem, just as they did in 'Introduction' (I). Now, however, the tears are of sadness, not of joy. The emmet imagines her children crying and the speaker cries too, out of pity and sympathy. The repeated 'w' sounds in stanza four represent the wailing of the distressed emmet. Tears and sighs recur throughout the *Songs*, reflecting the sadness of many of the characters and the unhappiness of the situations in which they find themselves.

In this case, however, the tears and darkness are not impenetrable. The speaker sleeps in 'an angel-guarded bed', and the glow-worm in the final two stanzas offers protection and hope to the emmet. She is not actually re-united with her children, but the final injunction to 'hie thee home' suggests that she will find her children safely there. The glow-worm provides light to contrast with and to chase away the surrounding darkness.

'The Little Girl Lost' and 'The Little Girl Found'

The opening two stanzas of 'The Little Girl Lost' (I) set Lyca's experiences in a biblical and global perspective. In a prophetic vision, the speaker describes the earth rising to return to its creator, and foresees a restoration of the earth to its initial paradisal state. This recalls both the Genesis creation story and the account of the end of time in Revelation, in which the old earth is replaced by a new and perfected creation: 'Then I saw a new heaven and a new earth, for the first had passed away' (Revelation 21:1). It also suggests the words of the prophet Isaiah: 'The desert and the parched land will be glad; the wilderness will rejoice with blossom. Like the crocus, it will burst into bloom; it will greatly rejoice and shout for joy' (Isaiah 35:1–2). The description of God as 'maker meek' contrasts with the concept of a powerful creator, but it is fully consistent with the image of Christ, God's earthly manifestation. This further suggests the connections Blake drew between apparent opposites.

The lion, whose regal nature is emphasised in both poems, also has biblical

connotations. Its 'mane of gold' in the first poem pre-empts the 'spirit armed in gold' of the second poem, and together with 'golden hair' and 'crown' links explicitly with apocalyptic visions of Christ. The lion's royal nature is underlined by the transformation of the 'caverns deep' of the first poem into the 'palace deep' of the second. As a wild beast, however, the lion initially appears to be a threat to Lyca.

It is possible to interpret this poem as being about innocence encountering sexual experience. The tree under which Lyca sleeps suggests the Tree of the Knowledge of Good and Evil in the garden of Eden, and in this respect Lyca can be seen to mirror Eve. The companion poem, 'A Little Girl Lost' (E), is about a father who forbids his daughter to enjoy natural and free love, which suggests that these poems may present an alternative state where such love can be enjoyed. (Blake was himself a theoretical advocate of free love, although he in fact remained faithful to his wife, Catherine.) There are a number of specific sexual overtones in the first poem: the lion licks Lyca's bosom and neck in stanza 11, and she is undressed by the lioness before being 'conveyed/To caves'. The lion's flaming eyes may suggest passion or even lust, and the 'Ruby tears' it sheds may represent the virgin blood of the ruptured hymen.

The paradisal imagery and the fact that the encounter takes place 'on hallowed ground' suggest that sexual experience is not incompatible with innocence. Yet the darkness evoked by the 'Frowning, frowning night' implies the fragility of innocence and the presence of threatening forces. As in 'A Dream' and many other poems, darkness and light coexist.

The isolation of Lyca and her parents is typical of that faced by many of the characters in the *Songs*, including the lone piper of 'Introduction' (I). The poem's wilderness location reflects this, as does the final image in the second poem of the restored family in 'a lonely dell'. 'The Little Girl Found', like 'A Dream', deals with the separation of parents and children. This might be a literal separation, but it could also be a figurative separation that occurs as a child, gaining independence, learns to face the problems of life alone. As in 'A Dream', the separation causes the parent(s) distress.

A further interpretation might be that the parents' search for the child may represent the 'journey' through sexual intercourse, leading to conception and, perhaps, a traumatic and difficult pregnancy. Lyca's wandering may represent the child's development through gestation, and her meeting with the lion and the wild beasts may suggest the dangers and pains of childbirth. Likewise, the 'Ruby tears' of the lion could represent the blood of childbirth, and the demands of labour would explain the mother's exhaustion and tears. This would offer an alternative explanation for the nakedness of Lyca at the end of the first poem and would set the final stanza of the second poem in a different light, as the new family returns home to start a new life together. This reading connects the poems to 'Infant Joy' and 'Infant Sorrow'.

'The Blossom'

This is another poem that seems simple, but on closer examination becomes more complex. The ambiguity of the identity of the poem's speaker, which becomes particularly important when considering the possessive pronoun 'my' in the last line of each stanza, adds to the complexity. If the speaker is the piper, it can be seen as a simple and innocent celebration of the natural world and the happy coexistence of the blossom, the robin and the sparrow. The title, with its suggestions of fruitfulness and promised growth, seems to support this. Similarly, if the blossom is the speaker, the poem can be seen to describe sympathy and interaction between elements of the natural world, which live symbiotically, supporting each other unawares.

The form of the poem is strikingly simple, even childlike, employing a closely repeated structure which reflects the apparent innocence of the subject matter. The second, third and sixth lines of each stanza are shared, while the first line of each stanza follows the same pattern. This is a trait the poem shares with both 'The Lamb' and 'Infant Joy', which deal with the related themes of new life.

However, a closer examination suggests a more complex and less innocent interpretation. 'The Blossom' can be seen as an exploration of innocent sexual awakening comparable to 'The Sick Rose' (E), which on one level deals with the destructive nature of sexual experience. Blake's illustration for 'The Blossom' supports this reading; the column of flame rising up the right-hand side of the page could be a phallic image, suggesting the blossoming of pubescent or pre-pubescent attraction. Blake's vocabulary seems to support this interpretation, too: the 'swift' movement of the sparrow and the 'sobbing' of the robin may suggest the varied emotions of love; the repeated word 'bosom' carries sexual connotations of breasts, while the apparently innocent searching for 'your cradle narrow' may suggest the vagina. The repeated phrase 'Near my bosom' implies secrecy, which is strengthened by the fact that the blossom appears to be hidden (or perhaps is hiding deliberately) 'Under leaves so green', and that it watches the approach of the sparrow and the robin from a place of concealment, as if awaiting the arrival of a lover.

'The Lamb'

As in 'The Blossom', Blake adopts a simple and repeated structure. In this poem, however, he adds a further dimension, using the first stanza to pose questions and the second stanza to answer them, a technique used in catechisms (a series of questions and answers used to instruct children in religious doctrine). This means that we can see the addressee of the poem as a lamb or as a little child. Whichever is the case, the opening stanza establishes an idyllic rural picture, recalling 'Introduction' (I), during which the piper is charged by the child-angel to 'Pipe a song about a lamb'. Everything in this stanza is perfection — 'delight', 'bright', 'Softest clothing' and 'tender voice'.

Stanza two answers the question of who created the lamb. Blake outlines the relationship between the lamb and Jesus in simple terms. In his use of 'meek' and 'mild' to describe Christ, he invokes a traditional picture, drawing particularly on the Christmas narrative of Christ's incarnation as a helpless baby. This image recalls the 'maker meek' from 'The Little Girl Lost' (I), linking the figure of the lamb to the powerful creator God. Finally Blake makes explicit the link between the lamb and Christian believers: 'I a child and thou a lamb,/We are callèd by his name.' Christians, whether adult or infant, are required to approach Christ as a child, reminding the reader of Christ's injunction that 'anyone who will not receive the kingdom of God like a little child will never enter it' (Luke 18:17). You should also refer to the analysis of 'The Tiger' (pp. 64–66), the contrary poem from the *Songs of Experience*.

'The Shepherd'

This poem smoothly follows 'The Lamb', allowing Blake to joke that the shepherd 'shall follow his sheep'. Blake's depiction of the shepherd, as for the lamb and the lion, is based on biblical sources (p. 21).

As in 'The Lamb', the reader is presented with an idyllic world. The use of the word 'strays' suggests a carefree existence, which allows the shepherd the time and space to praise his maker. Blake studiously avoids any but the most passing suggestion of trouble. This is an image of happy intimacy between the sheep and the shepherd, which mirrors that between God and Christian believers.

The poem also recalls the parenting theme explored in 'A Dream', 'The Little Girl Lost' (I) and 'The Little Girl Found' (I). At the beginning of stanza two the reader is presented with an ideal relationship between parent and child: 'For he hears the lamb's innocent call,/And he hears the ewe's tender reply.' This image of unity contrasts strongly with the images of separation found in the earlier poems.

'Infant Joy'

Another apparently simple poem, this seems to be a love song between a mother and a nameless 2-day-old baby. The poem emphasises happiness and love through the repetition of the word 'joy', which appears six times in the course of just 12 lines. The fact that the poem does not follow a regular metrical form might indicate the unrestrained, unbounded happiness of the mother with her new child.

There are other interpretations, however. Blake's illustration for the poem may lead the reader to see it as a poem about conception rather than about birth. It is possible that the conception or birth the poem explores is that of Jesus. The repetition of the phrase 'I am'/ 'I happy am' recalls the meeting between God and Moses in Exodus 3:14. When asked for his name by Moses, God replies: 'I am that I am… Thus shalt thou say unto the people, I am hath sent me unto you.' Similarly, the apostle John tells how Jesus, asserting his divine nature, said to the Pharisees: 'Before Abraham was, I am' (John 8:58).

The multiple meanings of the title makes a further reading possible. 'Infant Joy' can be taken to mean either the joy of the infant, the joy the parent takes in the infant, or a new joy. If the reader adopts the final view, the child becomes a metaphor for a new, joyful experience.

The preceding poems, however, suggest that 'Sweet joy' is by no means assured and that the 'innocence' of the newborn child will soon come under attack from the 'experience' of life.

'On Another's Sorrow'

This is a poem about sympathy — between parents and children, one person and another, God and mankind. The poem uses rhetorical questions, which draw us in and make us engage with the issues it raises. It includes numerous words associated with sadness: 'woe', 'sorrow', 'grief', 'tear', 'weep', 'groan', 'fear' and so on. These words are found repeatedly, not only throughout this poem, but throughout the *Songs* as a whole. In its focus on parental sorrow, the poem can be compared with 'A Dream' and 'The Little Girl' poems (I), as well as contrasting with the happiness of 'Infant Joy'.

The focus shifts in stanza four from human parents to God, the creator and parent of all. From this point, Blake emphasises God's caring and sympathetic nature:

- 'Are not two sparrows sold for a penny? Yet not one of them will fall to the ground apart from the will of your Father' (Matthew 10:29).
- 'Behold the fowls of the air: for they sow not, neither do they reap, nor gather into barns; yet your heavenly father feedeth them' (Matthew 6:26).

These echoes illustrate Blake's view of the extent to which God cares about his creation. His sympathy is evident when we see him 'Weeping tear on infant's tear'. Like the parent figures of 'A Dream' and the 'Little Girl' poems (to which it is linked metrically), and the shepherd in 'The Shepherd', Blake presents God as a caring and paternal figure who tends his creation 'night and day'. The image of God 'Wiping all our tears away' emphasises this.

This is not where Blake's presentation of God ends, however. In the final three stanzas of the poem he emphasises that God is not merely a sympathetic creator, but also has empathy with his creation. As in 'The Lamb', Blake draws on imagery of the incarnation of Christ and the nativity. This illustrates God's desire to know his creation, and when Blake refers to Christ as 'a man of woe' he recalls the prophet Isaiah's vision of Christ 'despised and rejected by men, a man of sorrows and familiar with suffering' (Isaiah 53:3–5).

This poem should also be compared with 'The Divine Image', which looks specifically at how mankind is a reflection of God and his characteristics.

'Spring'

In Blake's illustrated versions of the text, this poem is accompanied by a lavish and exuberant depiction of foliage. The riot of green leaves and the freedom of movement within the image suggest the freedom and joy of this poem. The remainder of the illustration depicts a small child and a lamb, recalling the triangle of Christ, child and lamb that Blake has already used on a number of occasions in the collection so far. Notice the striking number of references to poems that precede this one:

- 'Sound the flute!' ('Introduction' (I))
- 'Day and night' ('On Another's Sorrow')
- 'Little girl' ('The Little Girl Lost' (I) and 'The Little Girl Found' (I))
- 'Merry voice' ('Introduction' (I) and 'The Lamb')
- 'Infant noise' ('Infant Joy' and 'On Another's Sorrow')
- 'Little lamb' ('The Lamb')
- 'Come and lick/My white neck' ('The Little Girl Lost' (I))

As well as these explicit echoes of other poems, there are numerous other resonances. The verbal echoes demonstrate the carefully orchestrated use of vocabulary Blake employs in the *Songs*. He uses repeated words and phrases to reinforce his messages from one poem to the next, and to invoke images and concepts from earlier poems; this sophisticated technique adds considerably to the complexity of these apparently simple poems. This poem might be unmarked by the dark suggestions of many of the other poems in the collection, but the presence of images recurring from earlier poems makes the reader aware of the darkness that lurks beneath.

'The Schoolboy'

In a number of the combined editions of the *Songs*, Blake places this poem in the *Songs of Experience* section. This seems appropriate, given the emphasis on the drudgery of the schoolboy's experience in the classroom and the apparently damaging effect it has on him. The poem moves from carefree happiness and innocence to careworn sadness and experience; it begins with the delights of a 'summer morn' and the presence of music, both natural and man-made, and ends with the harshness of the 'blasts of winter' and the sounds of the raging storm.

The first stanza portrays a boy full of life and excitement. The idyllic rural setting, with singing birds and the distant sound of hunting horns on the warm summer air, paints a picture of simple happiness and of the boy in communion with the world around him. This changes when the issue of school is raised in stanza two. The partial repetition of the first line of the poem emphasises this change. Formal education 'drives all joy away'. Blake makes no comment on what the boy actually has to learn and whether this is good or bad, but rather focuses his attention on the figure of the schoolmaster, whose 'cruel eye outworn' seems to be the source of the boy's unhappiness and discomfort. This suggests that Blake wishes to criticise restrictive authority, rather than education itself — this is supported by the inferred strictness of the boy's parents, to whom he appeals in stanza five.

Stanza three develops the boy's response to his situation. Words such as 'drooping' and 'anxious' combine with the 'sighing and dismay' that ended the previous stanza, to emphasise the boy's emotions. 'Drooping' particularly conveys the image of a flower wilting in uncongenial conditions, and anticipates the flower imagery of stanza five. Like plants, children need nurturing. The boy appears to wish to enjoy the experience of his education: 'Nor in my book can I take delight,/Nor sit in learning's bower', but the implication is that he cannot; he is obstructed by the harsh schoolmaster.

Stanza four introduces the metaphor of a bird which, like that of the bud in the final two stanzas of the poem, is used to illustrate the boy's plight. The impact of formal schooling is far from a liberating and ennobling experience, becoming instead a source of despondency, which is emphasised by the repetition of 'droop'.

The fifth stanza begins with an appeal from the schoolboy to his parents. The schoolmaster is not the sole source of the boy's unhappiness and discomfort; both his parents and those *in loco parentis* are combining to ruin the 'springing day' of childhood. The boy protests that 'sorrow and care's dismay' should not be a part of the experience of childhood, which should be a time of innocent enjoyment. Blake's illustration for the poem depicts the childhood the schoolboy yearns for; it shows the child not only enjoying his book (notably out of the classroom), but also engaged in a game of marbles with his friends.

His restrictive education will mark the boy for the rest of his life: 'How shall the summer arise in joy,/Or the summer fruits appear?' The lurching of spring directly into the 'blasts of winter', with the richness of summer and the fruitfulness of autumn blighted, acts as a metaphor for the boy reaching old age having bypassed the joy of life. The poem presents a powerful picture of how the innocence of the child is forced into the unpleasant realities of experience by the thoughtlessness of unheeding adults.

'Laughing Song'

This is another simple lyric, which in its free combination of anapaestic and iambic feet seems to adopt the rhythm of laughter itself, reflecting the innocent joy the poem celebrates. The source of laughter and joy is the natural world, with the woods, the stream, the air, the hills, the meadows and the grasshopper all joining in. The human characters (represented by Mary, Susan and Emily) fit seamlessly into this joyous environment, and the vocabulary, with its repetition of 'laugh', 'merry' and 'sweet', adds to the general air of merriment.

The straightforward happiness and naive innocence of this poem contrast markedly with the darker notes struck by the preceding poem 'The Schoolboy', and 'The Little Black Boy' which follows. This indicates that, even in the midst of undesirable 'experience', innocent pleasure and laughter remain possible. In this respect, the poem is linked to 'The Blossom' and 'Spring'.

However, the surrounding poems in their turn suggest elements of darkness in 'Laughing Song'. A possible biblical reference to the prophet Isaiah undermines the innocence of the poem: 'But see, there is joy and revelry, slaughtering of cattle and killing of sheep, eating of meat and drinking of wine! "Let us eat and drink," you say, "for tomorrow we die!"' These words are echoed by Jesus in the parable of the rich fool in Luke 12:19. This is very different from the spirit of 'Laughing Song', but the verbal resonance hints at the dark shadows lurking beneath the poem's innocent surface.

'The Little Black Boy'

The social background to this poem, in which Blake tackles the issue of slavery and racial segregation, is explored on pp. 18–19. You should also refer to the sample essay on pp. 92–94. It is interesting that, for the first time in the *Songs*, Blake uses the iambic pentameter, which lends dramatic weight and dignity to the poem while retaining the rhythms of everyday speech.

In the first stanza, Blake uses the conventional associations of 'white' with good and 'black' with evil. The second and final lines of the stanza, however, quickly dispel the notion that Blake is reinforcing abhorrent views of race. On the contrary, he exploits these simple equations to point out the irony that underpins the poem — that the black boy is in many ways much 'whiter' than the white boy, who appears to be in the 'darkness' of ignorance. Blake's treatment of contraries suggests that distinctions of black and white are, if not false, at least open to debate. The black boy quickly informs us that although his skin is black, his soul is 'white', a message reinforced by the rest of the poem.

From stanza two the poem emphasises education, and should be compared to 'The Schoolboy'. Here education is undertaken in love; the kisses of the black boy's mother contrast strikingly with the apparently uninterested parents and the 'cruel eye' of the schoolmaster in the earlier poem. Similarly, the freedom of the open air and the location of the schoolroom under a tree contrasts with the suffocating imprisonment of the classroom in 'The Schoolboy'. The differences in the views of the two boys in the poem may be due to a difference in education — the black boy is noble, liberal and caring, while the hope he expresses at the end of the poem, that the white boy 'will then love me', suggests that the white boy holds the bigoted views current at the time. The mother's lesson is about faith; she teaches her son to see God as the source and the sustainer of his life, and the colour of his skin not as a burden but as proof of God's provision for him. The skin that protects the black boy from the sun is a blessing not afforded to the white boy, and the reader is therefore forced to reconsider the conventional values and attributes attached to black and white. The boy's mother also teaches him of the temporary nature of the physical body, which she refers to as 'but a cloud' carrying the soul within. The black boy, like all those who acknowledge the love of God, will become a lamb.

The final two stanzas proclaim the common humanity of black and white people. Both boys are lambs of God, even though this seems to be recognised only by the black boy. The white boy will not realise this, the black boy suggests, until death: 'When I from black and he from white cloud free.' The black boy is presented, in a bold reversal of contemporary views, as the more advanced, enlightened and 'Christian' of the two boys; it is he who will take on the role of protector and will, in an act of true grace and forgiveness, initiate reconciliation with the white boy who 'will then love me'.

Blake's message is bold and clear. Black and white are contraries, not opposites. Thus, for all the surface differences between the two boys, they remain essentially and spiritually bound to each other, and both, upon their deaths, will recognise the common humanity denied by the slave system.

'The Voice of the Ancient Bard'

This poem is marked by its prophetic and portentous tone. The term 'bard' calls to mind the Old Testament prophets; Blake alludes frequently to prophetic texts such as the books of Psalms, Isaiah, Daniel and Revelation, and here he takes on the prophetic voice himself (see pp. 25–28). If we assume that the previous poems have all been spoken by the less portentous (and possibly less authoritative) piper, this new voice marks a significant shift. The qualifying adjective 'ancient' suggests that this may be a figure of 'experience' rather than 'innocence', and in a number of the combined versions of the *Songs* Blake did indeed place this poem in the *Songs of Experience* section.

The opening call to the 'Youth of delight' may be a specific reference to 'The Little Black Boy', which precedes this poem. The black boy, like the youth in this poem, is called by a figure of authority to watch the coming of day (compare 'Look on the rising sun!' with 'see the opening morn'), and both youths are envisaged in a new dawn. Alternatively, it may be an invocation encompassing all youth, or a general appeal to any reader who is open to the dawning of 'truth new-born', a phrase which carries connotations of the nativity. The presence of dawn and new light is also connected to the opening of 'The Echoing Green', which follows.

Further links are suggested with 'The Little Black Boy' in lines four and five, where the bard refers to 'clouds of reason' and 'disputes', both of which play a central role in the preceding poem. Blake despised 'reason', which he saw as the enemy of human creativity. As 'The Little Black Boy' concludes, the flight of the undesirable ('reason', 'disputes' and 'teasing') heralds a better future.

However, darkness increases towards the end of the poem, as the victims of folly (the 'They' of line nine) stumble and fall, and seems to be asserting itself over the promised dawn of the opening of the poem. This looks forward to 'Earth's Answer' from the *Songs of Experience*, in which the new dawn appears to be over-whelmed by darkness, whereas the reference to 'Folly' calls to mind Proverbs 6, in which Solomon offers his warnings against folly. Like Solomon, Blake highlights its deceitful nature, a further threat to 'innocence'. The image of the bones of the dead (an allusion to the valley of the dry bones, told in Ezekiel 37) serves to deepen the darkness of the imagery.

For all the positive potential implicit in this poem, the reader is left with an image of negativity, as the bard describes a situation in which the blind are leading the blind in a world of darkness. The word 'leading' alludes to the image of the shepherd from previous poems, but Blake is quick to point out that in this case those who wish to lead should, in fact, be led. The bard seems to be warning the reader and the innocent against the dangers of false prophets, who will (wittingly or unwittingly) lead the foolish astray.

'The Echoing Green'

As in 'The Little Black Boy' and 'The Voice of the Ancient Bard', Blake uses imagery of the dawn and new light. In the previous two poems this is linked specifically to religious concepts; here, however, it serves two different functions: it establishes an atmosphere of happiness and freshness in the idyllic surroundings of the village green, and it suggests birth and the cycle of life. As in a number of other poems, such as 'Introduction' (I), 'Spring' and 'Laughing Song', there is repeated use of the vocabulary of happiness and merriment (e.g. 'happy', 'merry', 'cheerful', 'laugh'), suggesting the innocence of childish play and the happy memories of the adults. Blake employs short lines which speed the return of the rhyming sounds, keeping the idea of the echo firmly at the forefront of the reader's mind.

The first stanza presents a picture of natural harmony, as the bells, seasons, animals, plants and humans all join together to celebrate spring. The 'sports' of line nine suggests the innocent and energetic enjoyment of the children and their games that are accompanied, as if being endorsed by God, by the ringing of the church bells. The term 'echoing green' suggests nothing more, at this stage, than that the green echoes to the noises of the children at play, the sounds of nature and the pealing of the bells.

Stanza two introduces the elders of the village. Like the children, these old people are merry and unencumbered by 'care'. The relationship between the old and the young is evidently good; there is fellowship and sympathy between them. The old people recollect their own childhoods, seeing in the children at play an image of themselves when they were young; this deepens the meaning of the phrase 'the echoing green'.

The third stanza moves away from the innocent atmosphere of the first two. Blake makes it clear that childhood cannot and does not endure forever, any more than does the light of day, which begins to wane as the sun descends. As in 'Nurse's Song' (I), the children are allowed the freedom to play until dusk — which could be seen as symbolising the end of childhood — before they return to the parental fold. Blake presents this in ideal terms, picturing the children returning to their mothers 'Like birds in their nest'. The poem ends with the falling of darkness and 'the echoing green' becomes 'the darkening green'. This may simply be an evocation of the end of the day, but the ending of the sports and the connotations of the word 'darkening' can be read as sinister suggestions of the loss of innocence, or even encroaching death.

'Nurse's Song'

The opening line of this poem immediately establishes its connection with 'The Echoing Green'. Here, however, we see the events from the perspective of an adult rather than from that of a child. The prevailing atmosphere of the first stanza is carefree ('laughing', 'rest', 'still'); the nurse is tranquil and at peace because the children in her care are happy. The free combination of anapaestic and iambic feet maintains some of the joyful innocence of the previous poem, but introduces a discordant element to reflect the sense of increasing unease.

Unlike 'The Echoing Green', where darkness does not enter until the end of the poem, here it intrudes as early as lines 5 and 6. The phrase 'the dews of night arise' suggests an unhealthy and threatening atmosphere, and Blake's use of repetition ('Come, come', later repeated as 'No, no' and 'Well, well') suggests uneasy pleading.

In 'The Echoing Green', the children went willingly with their parents at nightfall. Here, however, they protest and beg to be allowed to play longer. This may represent the growth of the children and their developing sense of independence. Unlike the children in the preceding poem, they seem to be pushing at established boundaries.

The nurse's permission, granted at the beginning of stanza four, also suggests a development away from innocence and towards experience. The children no longer exist solely in the light, but are extending into the dusk of evening and towards night. The light that 'fades away' could therefore be seen as a symbol of fading childhood innocence. The nurse might then be sensibly allowing the children to mature and to take more responsibility for their own actions; alternatively, she might be guilty of exposing them to unwarranted risks. Another possibility is that she is aware of the pains of 'experience' that must follow in adolescence and adulthood, and so allows them to enjoy their innocent childhood games to the full. This interpretation is supported by the alliterative, liquid consonants of line 15, which might represent the children's laughter, but the heavy dactyl that ends the poem — the portentous 'echoèd' — has darker overtones.

This poem should be compared with 'Nurse's Song' (E), which provides a darker vision of childhood. Fruitful comparisons can also be made with 'The Garden of Love', where the 'green' of line four may be taken as the same green referred to by the nurse, a place no longer of permission and freedom, but of prohibition and restraint.

'Holy Thursday'

The social and political background to this poem can be found on pp. 18–19. Blake employs the unusual and heavy iambic heptameter, a seven-stress line, which contrasts starkly with the preceding poems and underlines the seriousness of his message.

The illustration accompanying this poem shows the children led in regimented fashion across the top and the bottom of the page. This contrasts sharply with the illustration accompanying 'The Echoing Green', where old and young mingle freely. The poem displays Blake's dislike of organised religion and its restrictive practices, which he saw as an impediment to knowing God fully. He also addresses this in 'The Garden of Love', and it can be compared to his dislike of restrictive formal education (seen in 'The Schoolboy' and 'The Little Black Boy') and reason (as in 'The Voice of the Ancient Bard').

Blake emphasises the innocence of the children attending the Holy Thursday service. He employs vocabulary that emphasises innocence (e.g. 'these flowers', 'radiance', 'lambs', 'innocent') and stresses the large number of children that are present (e.g. 'companies', 'thousands' 'multitude(s)'). The forceful use of such repetition urges us to question the social and economic conditions that give rise to such a mass reliance on charity. The use of the word 'lambs' is particularly powerful, simultaneously presenting the children as pure, innocent and defenceless creatures and also identifying them as sacrificial victims. Further biblical allusions include the phrases 'a mighty wind' and 'harmonious thunderings' (see p. 22).

The 'red and blue and green' of the children's school uniforms contrasts strikingly with the monochrome 'Grey headed beadles'. These men are in positions of authority, leading the procession of children, which recalls 'The Shepherd' and 'The Voice of the Ancient Bard', both of which also look at the concept of leading. Their white 'wands' are symbols of religious or educational authority, but can also be seen as instruments of chastisement and coercion. The invocation of the Thames reflects the great tide of poverty represented in this flowing 'river' of charity-school children.

The 'agèd men' sit 'beneath' the children. This may imply the physical layout of the cathedral for the service, where the old men (supposedly wise and worthy of respect) are seated in the more honoured seats on the main floor of the church, below the children, who sit on the balcony. Alternatively, it may imply that these men, for all their social importance, are morally and spiritually 'beneath' the children, whose innocence and value is beyond question. The term 'wise guardians' can be seen either as straightforward praise, or as cutting sarcasm, depending upon the reader's interpretation of the poem.

The final line refers to the story in Genesis 18–19, when Abraham welcomes three strangers into his house, thereby showing them true charity, and later discovers that his guests were angels. The apostle Paul refers to this in Hebrews, encouraging the members of the congregation to display true charity to their fellow humans. True 'pity', if one sees this as an ironic poem, is what appears to be lacking in the treatment of society's most vulnerable members.

'The Divine Image'

This poem is influenced by the teachings of Swedenborg, whose ideas are explained in more detail on pp. 29–31, and explores the relationship between God and humans.

Blake begins with a list of admirable abstract qualities. 'Mercy, Pity, Peace and Love' have been referred to repeatedly in the course of the *Songs* so far, though rarely in an unchallenged or untainted form. Blake refers to them as 'virtues of delight', emphasising their godly value. He goes on to locate these qualities within both God and mankind, and in stanza three applies them to the human body. Blake's apparently simple equation is questionable, however, given the repeated failure of humans to display such characteristics.

Blake explores Swedenborg's idea of Christ as a divine human, suggesting that God is found in every person. This is implied by the repetition of the word 'every' in stanza four, the use of 'all' in stanza five, and the universality of 'In heathen, Turk or Jew'. The insistence that whoever 'prays in his distress,/Prays to the human form divine' and the ensuing demand that therefore 'all must love the human form' cements the message. Any act of cruelty and disrespect, or failure to demonstrate care and love, is an act of sin committed not only against a human being, but against God himself.

The end of the poem recalls 'The Little Black Boy', as Blake appeals for racial and religious tolerance. Humans must respect the image of God in each other, regardless of apparent differences and divisions.

'The Chimney-Sweeper'

It might seems strange that a poem set in the harsh and unforgiving world of experience should be included in the *Songs of Innocence*. However, this might be explained by the fact that it is told from the 'innocent' perspective of the child. Although the poem looks in detail at the harsh realities of life for the boys who worked as sweeps, there is a note of innocent hope that the companion poem in the *Songs of Experience* lacks. Blake employs lines with alternating anapaestic and iambic feet, giving a surprisingly light and almost cheerful air; perhaps this innocent tone is intended to underline the irony of this very serious poem.

Blake begins by emphasising the speaker's isolation — he is motherless, and has been sold by his father to a chimney-sweep. The overtones of slavery here are significant, especially when we consider that, since he is blackened by soot, this sweep is another little black boy. Blake emphasises how young he is through his inability to properly pronounce the word 'sweep' ('weep weep weep weep') — a pun which also picks up on the boy's sadness and tears. The pathos is enhanced in stanza two through the comparison of the boy's hair with lamb's wool. The boy suffers having his head shaved in silence; apart from being a sign of degradation, the incident alludes to the words of the prophet Isaiah, foreshadowing of the brutal treatment of Christ leading up to his crucifixion:

> He was oppressed and afflicted, yet he did not open his mouth; he was led like a lamb to the slaughter, and as a sheep before her shearers is silent, so he did not open his mouth.
>
> (Isaiah 53:7).

The vision described in stanzas three to five recalls other visions in the *Songs of Innocence*, for example in 'Introduction' (I), 'A Dream', 'The Little Black Boy' and 'The Voice of the Ancient Bard'. Tom Dacre's vision of thousands of boys recalls the 'multitudes' of charity children from 'Holy Thursday' and illustrates the extent of the social evil Blake is exposing here. The image of the boys 'locked up in coffins of black' refers to their chimney environment, but also underlines the deadly nature of their occupation and their inability to escape from their plight.

The appearance of the angel in the fourth stanza is an image of salvation and liberation, suggesting the end of the world and the raising of the dead. This is followed by images of freedom and childhood play similar to the idyllic world of 'The Echoing Green'. The final line of the stanza relies heavily on the symbolism of baptism and purification, ideas which are developed in the fifth stanza, in which the angel teaches the children, freed now from the drudgery of work ('their bags left behind'), how to live with God as their father — a father who will not sell them into the slavery of sweeping. Words such as 'naked', 'white' and 'clouds' suggest purity, and echo 'The Little Black Boy'. This is a vision of hope, and the innocent Tom Dacre goes to work the next morning 'happy and warm' in spite of the awful conditions and dark future he faces.

The final line of the poem is somewhat problematic, and is open to a number of interpretations:

- It could be read as a suggestion that the sweeps and others like them should passively accept their lot, doing their duty whatever the conditions in the certainty that they will be rewarded in heaven. This interpretation sits uneasily with Blake's own strong views on social justice and the apparent sympathy he has for the sweeps.
- It might be a deeply ironic summary of this social evil, a pious moral truism, allowing those in more favoured circumstances to avoid a more uncomfortable moral duty. In this case, 'all' and 'they' both apply to the child sweeps.

■ It could be taken more radically as a call on those in authority, as well as those who buy and employ the child sweeps ('all'), to do their duty and bring this practice to an end, so that the boys ('they') will cease to suffer.

'A Cradle Song'

This is another poem exploring the relationship between a mother and a newborn infant. It can be compared with 'Infant Joy', and also with 'The Lamb' and 'The Divine Image' (I), all of which deal with Blake's understanding of the relationship between humanity and Christ (see pp. 30–31).

It is Blake's use of close verbal parallels between the opening two lines of this poem and lines 13–14 of 'The Human Abstract' which is most striking, however. It suggests that the innocent baby, later explicitly identified with Christ, faces a future where the 'shades' of parental protection will be replaced by the more threatening 'shades' of original sin and experience.

As the poem progresses, however, such overtones are borne away in a stream of images of innocence — the poet invokes 'pleasant streams', similar to the brook of 'Introduction' (I), but contrasting with the Thames in both 'Holy Thursday' (I) and 'London'. The 'mother's smiles' protect the infant through the darkness of the 'night' (the title of the last poem in the *Songs of Innocence* and a potent image of threat elsewhere). Words that are generally a sign of sadness and experience, such as 'moans' and 'sighs', are modified by the presence of the adjectives 'sweet' and 'dovelike', to highlight the child's innocent, untroubled slumber.

The repetition of words such as 'sweet', 'sleep' and 'smiles' creates an idealised picture of parental love and childhood innocence. Blake uses long, yawning vowel sounds ('down', 'crown', 'delight', 'beguiles', 'moans', 'creation' etc.) to reflect the child's sleepiness and perhaps recreate the sound of the mother's lullaby. The alternating metrical structure (iamb/anapaest followed by anapaest/iamb/iamb results in a gently rocking rhythm, perhaps suggesting the mother's steady rocking of the infant's cradle.

In the fifth stanza, the poem moves away from the specific and turns to the universal, when the mother observes that 'All creation slept and smiled'. As in 'The Lamb', Blake draws detailed parallels between the child and Christ.

'The Little Boy Lost' and 'The Little Boy Found'

These two poems should be read in conjunction. There is a strong contrast between the earthly father of the first poem and the heavenly father of the second poem. The poems could be read in the following ways:

■ The earthly father deliberately leaves his child behind, abandoning him to face the dangers of the world alone. This contrasts with the heavenly father of the second poem who, like the good shepherd, comes in search of the missing child or lamb.

- The earthly father (a sinful and flawed human being) misleads his child through poor parenting. The son later manages to overcome this with the help of the heavenly father.
- The earthly father abandons his household and children (like the father in 'The Chimney-Sweeper (I)).
- There is a breakdown in the relationship between a father and his son.
- This is an account of a bereavement, the son losing his way in the wake of the death of his father.

'The Little Boy Lost'

Blake emphasises the earthly father's uncommunicative nature, whether as a result of malice, poor parenting, or death. In spite of the son's pleas that he slow down and that he 'speak', the father remains aloof, unwilling or unable to communicate, and offers no assistance to his struggling and vulnerable son. The second stanza depicts the child lost in the dark, drenched in dew and weeping in the deep and dangerous mire, symbols of the more abstract dangers and uncertainties that surround him.

The final image of the disappearing vapour appears to be threatening, even malignant, suggesting perhaps a spiritual presence or a will-o'-the-wisp — in Blake's illustration this is exactly the form that the father takes. If we read this as a poem about the father's death, it may represent the departure of his soul.

'The Little Boy Found'

This poem begins where the previous one ended, with the little boy wandering lost in the fens. The strange will-o'-the-wisp-like figure has now become 'the wand'ring light', perhaps alluding to the story of the Israelites wandering in the desert after their liberation from Egypt, when 'By day the Lord went ahead of them in a pillar of cloud to guide them on their way and by night in a pillar of fire to give them light' (Exodus 13:21). The good intentions and true guidance of God, however, are distinctly at odds with the misleading light of the earthly father, underlining the irony of Blake's allusion.

There are also literary sources for these 'spirits of the air'. The most direct is from Milton's *Paradise Lost*, when Satan leads Eve into temptation (see pp. 31–32). Shakespeare's plays provide two more sources. The first is the character of Puck in *A Midsummer Night's Dream*, who takes great pleasure in deliberately misleading wayfarers, sometimes at his own volition and sometimes under orders from Oberon, the king of the fairies. The other is Ariel from *The Tempest*, a character who has much in common with Puck; under Prospero's control he takes on a variety of forms, corporeal and non-corporeal, to lead (and mislead) the people Prospero has brought to his island. The misleading, possibly malign, spirit of the earthly father contrasts strongly with the shepherd-like heavenly father, who kisses the child paternally and

leads him to his mother by the hand. The figure of the searching mother in this poem recalls similar characters in 'A Dream' and the 'Little Girl' (I) poems.

'Night'

This poem offers a picture of peace and calm at the end of the *Songs of Innocence*, a fond farewell to the collection. Each stanza divides into two quatrains (sets of four lines), the first made up of regular iambs, the second of anapaests. The effect of this is to make the first half of each stanza read more ponderously than the second half, which is lighter in tone. The 'silent delight' of the moon casts a benevolent light on the world, and words such as 'flower', 'bower' and 'smiles' create a sense of harmony and safety. The air of happy innocence appears to continue with the presence of the 'angels bright' and their blessings of sleep.

These appearances should not be accepted without question, however. Blake's language creates a distinct sense of unease: the farewell to 'green fields and happy groves' arouses the uncomfortable suspicion that such idyllic surroundings will have little to do with the world of experience that the reader is about to encounter. This impression is heightened by the past-tense phrases 'have took delight' and 'have nibbled', which suggest that these activities might no longer continue.

However, these threatening overtones are not new; the distress of many of the characters that inhabit the world of 'innocence' should be remembered. Stanza four returns to the more threatening world of wild beasts, recalling the 'Little Girl' (I) poems and prefiguring 'The Tiger' of *Experience*. The angels of 'Night' do not have unlimited powers — death and violence are part of, not opposite to, Blake's perception of the state of 'innocence'; where they cannot provide earthly safety, however, they do usher in 'New worlds', suggesting the movement of the soul from earth to heaven (see Revelation 21:1), a suggestion taken up at the end of stanza five, where the lion envisages the night of the poem's title transformed into 'immortal day'.

The lion and the lamb, biblical symbols of Christ, represent contraries. As they come together, so good and evil, safety and danger, protection and abandonment conjoin within the state of innocence. The unification of these contraries in the divine person of Jesus results in perfection — 'Wrath by his meekness,/And by his health sickness,/Is driven away'. In a fulfilment of Isaiah's famous prophesy, lines 41–42 show the wild beast lying down with the lamb (Isaiah 11:6). The concluding imagery of baptism has a biblical echo too.

'Night', and the *Songs of Innocence*, end on a slightly ambiguous note. While the overall message is of unity and safety in 'the fold', where the innocent are guarded by Christ, the lion, Blake alerts the reader to the coming of 'experience'. This poem asserts Blake's views on Christ's character, but also makes the reader aware that Christ's protection does not preclude the possibility of violence, nor does 'innocence' prevent the incursion of 'experience'.

Songs of Experience

'Introduction'

'Introduction' (E) and 'Earth's Answer' are a complex pair of poems and introduce the reader suddenly to the harsh and disturbing world of the *Songs of Experience*, a world radically different from, but at the same time integrally connected to, the world of the *Songs of Innocence*. They should be read in conjunction, since some of their difficulties can be clarified by comparing the two.

A comparison of 'Introduction' with that from the *Songs of Innocence* reveals verbal echoes, such as the repetition of 'wat'ry shore', that emphasise how closely the poems are connected. The merry lightness of the earlier 'Introduction' has been lost; the piper's melodious voice is replaced by the discordant strains of the 'voice of the bard', and the uneasy lurches in rhythm reflect the profound sense of unhappiness. Similarly, the virginal natural world is supplanted by a vision of a sloth-like and weary earth of 'ancient trees' and 'fallen, fallen light'. The voice of 'The Holy Word' (see pp. 23–24), which should be the inspiration of mankind, cuts a very different figure from the angel-child that inspires the piper. This poem, however, adopts a more threatening tone, opening with a resounding imperative: 'Hear the voice of the bard!' This impression of authority is strengthened as the bard claims omniscience ('Who present, past and future sees') and direct connection with God ('Whose ears have heard/The Holy Word').

Blake usually refers to God as 'the Holy Word' to emphasise his power as a creator. However, this contrasts with the portrayal of God in this poem, as Blake depicts him wandering among the trees — an image that recalls Genesis 3:8–24, in which God walks in the Garden of Eden searching for his fallen creation. God is shown suffering in the face of 'experience', as his beloved creation proves flawed. His tears are an important image: they might express sympathy for 'the lapsèd soul'; sorrow that the lapse has occurred; or frustration in the face of an opposing power (in this tale, Satan, although he is not referred to directly). '[T]he ancient trees' that God wanders among suggests that the poem is not set in the fresh, new Eden of the creation story, although the modifier 'ancient' may simply be referring back to the beginning of the world.

A key element of the poem's complexity stems from a grammatical ambiguity. The phrase 'That might control' has been the topic of much critical debate, the question being whether it is the bard, the Holy Word (i.e. God) or the lapsèd soul (i.e. mankind) who controls the 'starry pole'. Whatever the interpretation, the image of the 'starry pole' suggests hope (Milton uses these words to describe the night sky watched by Adam and Eve prior to the fall of man in *Paradise Lost*), as does the concept of renewed light.

The message of the final stanza is ambiguous, too. The phrases 'starry floor' and 'wat'ry shore' both imply a form of limitation. One interpretation is that God is reassuring humans that although they are currently living in night, and bound to the earth and the shore, this is not an eternal punishment. Hope is offered by the promise of 'the break of day', which could symbolise the coming of Christ. An alternative interpretation could be that the limitations suffered by the Earth may be seen to endure until the new dawn of the second coming, a much less comforting possibility.

'Earth's Answer'

This poem shares the same varied form and metre as 'Introduction' (E), which reinforces the connections between the two poems. In allowing Earth a voice to answer God's judgement, Blake follows a format from the Bible, in which men are allowed to reply to God's words. For example, Abraham pleads for the cities of Sodom and Gomorrah (Genesis 18); Moses pleads for the people of Israel after they have forged the golden calf (Exodus 32); and Job argues with God over the treatment he receives at the hands of his enemies.

This poem has a number of possible interpretations depending on the reader's view of the ending of 'Introduction'. If God's message is one of hope, then Earth's response seems ungrateful, tainted by sin and 'experience'. If, on the other hand, God's message is a Blakean nightmare of 'reason' and stunted creativity, then Earth's response is understandable.

The poem opens in a profoundly dark mood, the image of Earth lying prone, suggesting vulnerability and despair. The alliteration of the consonant 'd' ('raised', 'head', 'darkness', 'dread', 'drear', 'fled', 'covered', 'despair') has a percussive and dulling effect. Earth is a female figure, placing her in direct contrast to the male figure of God. This may suggest the unity that should exist between the earth and its creator — throughout Revelation, the church is seen as the 'bride' of Christ. Alternatively, it may suggest the differences between Earth and God, which become more apparent as the poem progresses. The bountiful imagery associated with Mother Earth is replaced by the monochrome 'grey' of her hair, suggesting age and lack of vitality. 'Stony dread' heralds the frigidity of the response to come.

This dichotomy of 'masculine' and 'feminine' characteristics could indicate the dominance of God and the enforced passivity of Earth. Earth seems to view God as a figure resembling Urizen, one of Blake's mythological characters (see pp. 78–79), who embodies jealousy, 'reason' and restriction.

In one of many images of reduction, the bountiful imagery associated with Mother Earth is reduced to the monochrome 'grey' of her hair, suggesting old age and a lack of vitality. The heaven implied by the 'starry pole' in the preceding poem is reduced to 'Starry jealousy', thereby transforming a place of ideal rest and liberty to one of restriction. This use of 'jealousy' evokes Old Testament portrayals of God — in Exodus, God proclaims: 'I, the Lord your God, am a jealous God, punishing

the children for the sins of the fathers to the third and fourth generation of those who hate me.' But Earth omits that he also shows love 'to a thousand generations of those who love me and keep my commandments' (Exodus 20:5–6), reducing God from a figure of benevolent power to a figure 'Cold and hoar'.

Earth's harsh accusations towards God ('Selfish! Vain!/Eternal bane!') demonstrate that God is not only the meek and humble figure of the *Songs of Innocence*, but that he also has an altogether different side — a holy nature that cannot abide the sins of humanity and that exacts punishment for disobedience. The contraries of God's nature are neatly summarised in the final line of the poem: 'That free love with bondage bound'. The God of 'Introduction' (E) and 'Earth's Answer' is very different to the God of 'The Lamb' or 'The Shepherd'. However, the humanity of these poems is also a different humanity — it is not the humanity of innocent childhood, but humanity degraded and stripped of its innocence.

'The Clod and the Pebble'

This poem presents two opposing views of love, voiced by a clod and a pebble. The properties of the clod (a soft lump of clay) and the pebble (a hard stone) are significant, and it might be argued that the poem favours the pebble's harder, more selfish views. This is supported by the poem's structure, which gives the pebble's views second, allowing it to counter the clod's views and leaving its argument in the reader's mind. However, such a straightforward reading might not be appropriate, as the poem may well be meant ironically.

The first stanza offers an idealised view of love, though whether the subject is fraternal love, parental love, sexual love or the love that exists between friends is not made clear. The reader could therefore take the poem to be about 'love' in the abstract. The views presented by the clod have much in common with the biblical idea of love. Its definition concludes by expressing the power of genuine, selfless love, indicating that it can overcome evil to '[build] a Heaven in Hell's despite'. The fact that the speaker is a lowly clod of clay 'Trodden with the cattle's feet' may suggest the humility that is necessary for true love; however, it is also possible to see the low and degraded position of the clod as a denigration of the views it expresses.

The pebble's views contrast sharply with those of the clod, and offer a rebuttal of the biblical paradigm of love. Blake's presentation of the pebble's views seems to be the more attractive; where the clod 'sang' its message, the pebble 'warbled' its words in 'metres meet', the word 'meet' suggesting that its ideas are seemly or proper. However, this might be read as being deeply ironic, exposing how selfish and wrong the pebble's views are.

The concept of imprisonment recurs in this poem, continuing the theme from 'Earth's Answer', in which Earth is imprisoned by the apparently selfish love of God. Far from offering liberty and 'ease' (the results of love according to the clod), the purpose of the selfish love proclaimed by the pebble is 'To bind another to its delight'. Curiously, both types of love appear, in their own ways, to be constructive. Both succeed in building, although the selfish love of the pebble builds a damaging 'Hell in Heaven's despite'. The regular iambic tetrameter, a rather plodding metre, provides a sombre accompaniment to the debased image of love with which the poem concludes.

'Holy Thursday'

For background information on the Holy Thursday church service at St Paul's Cathedral, see p. 18.

Unlike the companion poem in the *Songs of Innocence*, Blake's views are presented here without ambiguity. The contrast with 'Holy Thursday' (I) is clear from the outset, as the 'children walking two and two' have been transformed into 'Babes reduced to misery'. The children appear from the outset as vulnerable innocents thrown into the jaws of 'experience'. Similarly, the 'wise guardians of the poor' of the former poem have here become the 'usurous hand'. Blake's use of synecdoche dehumanises the dispensers of charity; represented as a hand only, they conspicuously lack either mind or heart in their treatment of the children. Moreover, since usury is the lending of money at extortionate rates of interest, a practice condemned by the Bible (Nehemiah 5:10 urges 'But let the exacting of usury stop'), the reference implies the heavy price the 'babes' of the poem are forced to pay for the charity they receive — Blake's rhetorical questioning of the 'holiness' of this makes his views abundantly clear. The fact that these children exist 'In a rich and fruitful land' increases their plight. It recalls the famous line from *Milton*, better known as part of the hymn 'Jerusalem', describing 'England's green and pleasant land'; in both cases, the wealth of the land finds its way to the few.

Instead of the 'mighty wind' and 'harmonious thunderings' of song heard in 'Holy Thursday' (I), here the reader strains to hear the 'trembling cry' raised by the children. As holiness was lacking from stanza one, so the happy praise of the children is missing from stanza two. The 'rich and fruitful land' is transformed in this stanza into 'a land of poverty'. This poverty, Blake seems to imply, is not economic, but is a lack of true charity, conscience and love, ideas which link closely to the discussion of selfless and selfish love expressed in 'The Clod and the Pebble'.

The repeated 'their' of stanza three refers to the 'babes' of the opening stanza. This points out the increasing distinction between the children and the 'hand' of charity — a 'them and us' mentality. In the children's world, 'sun' and the fruits of harvest are absent, recalling the complaint of Earth in stanza four of 'Earth's Answer'. Like Earth, trapped by 'this heavy chain/That does freeze my bones around', the children of charity are forced to endure an 'eternal winter'.

The fourth stanza employs a pair of significant puns, both of which return to ideas established in the *Songs of Innocence*. Blake's play on 'sun'/'son' and

'rain'/'reign' invokes Christ. Wherever the 'sun' and 'rain' are found, the harvest will be plentiful; equally, wherever Christ the 'son' of God 'reigns', there will be no spiritual poverty. The importance of these ideas is reinforced through the harvest images in stanza three. The presence of Christ in these innocent children and the apparent absence of his presence in the 'usurous hand' of the charitable guardians is at the root of this poem. The metrical shifts, which often occur at the end of a stanza, emphasise this uneasy contrast.

'The Chimney-Sweeper'

For the social context to this poem, see pp. 18–19.

Unlike Tom Dacre in the companion poem from *Songs of Innocence*, this child (nameless and depersonalised in this case) has a worldly and cynical outlook. Perhaps Blake intends the reader to see in this boy an older and harder version of Tom Dacre.

Blake's use of black and white is significant. The sweep is described as 'A little black thing among the snow'. This image simultaneously dehumanises the sweep, reducing him to an unspecified black object, and makes him vulnerable, threatened by the cold (a comparison can be drawn with the 'eternal winter' of 'Holy Thursday' (E) and freezing bones of Earth in 'Earth's Answer'). The boy attributes his sale directly to his happiness and smiles, which suggests that he has been sold to spite his carefree 'innocence'. The image of the boy 'happy upon the heath' recalls fleetingly the atmosphere of 'The Echoing Green', but he is soon exposed to the hardships of 'experience' and forced to move from the pleasures of childhood, symbolised by the 'winter's snow', into the trials of the adult world, represented by the black 'clothes of death'.

The cry of 'weep, weep' echoes Tom Dacre's cry, but here the song is given added poignancy, because it is sung 'in notes of woe'. This establishes the child as a pathetic and unhappy figure, akin to the chimney sweep in 'London', where 'marks of woe' are found everywhere. It might be that the two sweeps are the same person.

The boy's parents are presented unfavourably. The possibility that they have gone to church to pray because of a sense of guilt and shame for selling their son as a sweep is undermined as the poem progresses. Because their son still dances and sings (presumably in an attempt to hide his sadness), they 'think they have done me no injury'. They seem to be deliberately turning a blind eye to reality and to the needs of their child. The parents use the child's apparent happiness to justify their continued exploitation of him. This is consistent with the religious hypocrisy implied at the end of the poem, as the parents 'praise' God, presumably for their new-found source of income. Profoundly suspicious of organised religion, Blake ends the poem by focusing on the contraries of 'heaven' and 'misery' in a phrase similar to that in 'The Clod and the Pebble'. The parents of the chimney-sweeper have, through their own selfishness, built a hell for their child.

'Nurse's Song'

This poem is darker and more sombre than its partner poem in the *Songs of Innocence*. The opening line and the structure of the stanzas are identical, a technique which underlines the differences between the two poems. The difference in atmosphere becomes apparent in the second lines of the poems: the 'laughing…heard on the hill' is replaced with 'whisperings…in the dale'; the physical contrast between the height of the hills and the depth of the dale signals a movement from innocence to experience. The laughter of the first poem is associated with children and their games, but the whisperings of the second poem are far more ambiguous. They may be the voices of the children, suggesting secrecy and conceal-ment, or they may be the voices of worldly temptations, or the plots of those seeking to corrupt the children's innocent minds.

Perhaps the most significant difference is the absence of any voice other than the nurse's. Whereas the previous poem is a dialogue between the nurse and her charges, here the only other voices are the 'whisperings' of line two. The precise nature of the nurse's embittered memories remains uncertain. The reader is left in doubt as to whether the 'green' and pallor of her countenance is a nauseous reaction to bad memories or something more complex, perhaps a combination of fear (pallor) and jealousy ('green').

Blake's original illustration emphasises the nurse's dominance. In the first poem she is challenged by the children, but, in keeping with her position in the second poem, she is placed in the centre of the image, she towers over a boy, while a girl sits in a doorway, as if she is on the threshold of 'experience'. Both children seem lifeless, but the rioting branches that swirl around the text of the poem and the rich clusters of grapes suggest the tempting energy of the world of 'experience' and its forbidden fruits awaiting them on the other side of the door.

The second stanza opens with another repetition of 'Nurse's Song' (I), but with a significant alteration in the punctuation. Line five of the first poem is punctuated at the caesura with a colon, indicating that the nurse's instruction to her charges to come home stems from a desire to protect them from the falling of night with its threatening 'dews'. The second poem, however, punctuates the caesura with a comma, implying that this protective instinct is much reduced or even absent. This important difference may well arise from the nurse's complex emotions. Lines seven and eight present a blighted view of childhood; the idea that 'Your spring and your day are wasted in play' flatly contradicts the schoolboy's feelings in 'The Schoolboy', who wishes for play rather than formal education. The nurse's description of childhood as 'your winter and night in disguise' suggests that the 'innocence' of childhood is a sham.

'The Sick Rose'

There are many possible interpretations of 'The Sick Rose'. It is ostensibly a simple poem about destructive nature, but a closer inspection reveals the darker meanings

of the world of 'experience' and sexual love. The poem is formed from a single sentence, which creates a sense of inevitable movement from the opening statement to the conclusion. It can be compared with 'The Blossom', which also arguably deals with nascent sexuality, and with other poems dealing with sexual experience, such as the 'Little Girl' (I and E) poems. The rose was the medieval symbol for female chastity and virginity, and is traditionally seen as representative of romantic love, which is conspicuously lacking in the poem. The worm, a creature associated with destruction and decay, also has phallic connotations.

The illustration that accompanies the poem (see p. 14) depicts a closed rose. A worm penetrates the flower at the same time as another figure leaves it, perhaps suggesting the death of the rose, the loss of innocence or the loss of virginity, which would pun on the idea of deflowering. The text is surrounded by briars, which may represent the threat the rose faces. In the top left-hand corner a caterpillar feeds on the foliage (see also 'The Human Abstract'), which adds to the oppressive sense of danger in the poem.

The clear statement with which the poem begins is followed by images of concealment and threat. The worm is all the more disturbing given that it is 'invisible', making the threat more subversive and potent. This is not a slow, creeping creature, but an airborne worm that 'flies in the night', an embodiment of evil operating under the cover of night (there might be further sexual over-tones here). The fourth line adds to the uneasy atmosphere, as the 'howling storm' seems to indicate powerful forces out of control, surrounding and buffeting the fragile flower.

The second stanza follows without a break from the first. Throughout the poem, Blake employs enjambment to create the momentum that drives the rose, the worm and the reader towards the conclusion (or consummation). The fifth line's pun on the word 'bed', referring to a flowerbed and the bed of sexual experience, supports a sexual interpretation of the poem, as does the double meaning of the following line, where the 'crimson joy' could refer to the rich colour of the rose's petals, or to the blood of lost virginity. The final emphasis on the 'dark secret love' of the worm, with its return to the concepts of concealment and darkness, reiterates the threat of 'experience' and its ultimately destructive nature, whether it is specif-ically sexual or more general. 'Joy' and 'life', two of the watchwords of the *Songs of Innocence,* cannot survive the 'howling storm'.

'The Fly'

Flies are frequently associated with disease and death. They also have evil connota-tions, primarily through the figure of Beelzebub, the lord of the flies. In 'The Human Abstract', the fly feeds on the 'Mystery' of human nature, suggesting the presence of dark psychological forces. Here, however, the fly appears to be a more benign presence.

The simplicity of the verse structure in this poem (a two foot iambic line) resembles a nursery rhyme. This might reflect the simple ideas in the poem, or suggest that they are reductive and naive. The illustration that accompanies it initially seems to have no discernible link to the poem's content. It portrays a mother (or perhaps a nurse) with two children in her care. The woman is helping the younger child, a boy, to walk — perhaps he has been 'damaged' by the hand of providence, or maybe his 'wing' has been 'brushed' in the same way as Blake envisages in the poem. The second child is an older girl who plays alone at shuttlecock. It could be that the shuttlecock is actually an outsized fly, which it closely resembles, about to be struck and damaged as described in the poem.

The image also resembles the illustration to 'Nurse's Song' (E), a poem to which 'The Fly' has interesting links. 'Nurse's Song' (E) — and 'The Schoolboy', where 'the joys of summer' appear an impossibility to the disenchanted child — suggests that summer is a brief and vulnerable season, which can be thoughtlessly brushed away. Like summer, the life of the fly is presented as fragile; Blake seems to use this as a metaphor for human existence or happiness, recalling Gloucester's line in *King Lear*: 'As flies to wanton boys are we to the gods,/They kill us for their sport' (IV.1.38–39).

Blake creates a simple (perhaps even depressingly simplistic) picture of human existence: 'For I dance/And drink and sing'. These lines recall 'The Chimney-Sweeper' (E), in which dancing and singing mask the terrible reality of life. This also suggests that the 'summer's play' of the fly is not as carefree and innocent as it may at first appear. In addition, Blake's words ominously echo those of the prophet Isaiah: 'But see, there is joy and revelry, slaughtering of cattle and killing of sheep, eating of meat and drinking of wine! "Let us eat and drink," you say, "for tomorrow we die!"'

This lurking presence of death is significant within 'The Fly', as is the 'hand' that dispenses it. The 'thoughtless hand' and the 'blind hand' of the poem recall the 'usurous hand' of 'Holy Thursday' (E). This hand could be the hand of God, if we take the fly as a metaphor for humanity. If this is the case, the reader is confronted with the dark, disturbing image of God presented in 'Earth's Answer', as the word 'blind' implies an arbitrary dispensation of death. We are obliged to consider whether the poem's resigned (and apparently cheerful) acceptance of death can be taken at face value.

'The Angel'

Useful comparisons can be made between this poem and 'A Poison Tree', for its focus on deceit, and with 'My Pretty Rose Tree' and 'The Lily', when considering it as a love poem.

The poem is set in the familiar Blakean world of dreams and visions. The angel (or lover) who appears to the narrator is a figure of benevolence and peace. The final

line of stanza one, however, makes it clear that she will reject him. This is a complex line, but it seems that the woman has become prey to 'Witless woe' — senseless sadness. This may be the sadness that is explored in the course of stanza two, which eventually leads to the flight of the angel at line nine. If so, the woman's observation that 'Witless woe was ne'er beguiled' suggests that her foolishness has indeed beguiled — or tricked — her, and robbed her of her angel.

Stanza two is similar to the second stanza of 'A Poison Tree'. Both poems deal with the destructive nature of secrecy and the sadness that arises from it. Here the woman's reluctance to accept the comfort offered by the angel leads to her unwillingness to share her 'heart's delight' — perhaps this means she kept her love from him. Her deceit leads directly to the flight of the angel/lover.

The breaking of the dawn heralds a new phase in the relationship. However, Blake seems to invert its usual connotations of hope; the red dawn light could be seen as a warning. The woman perversely dries her eyes and prepares herself to do battle with the very person who has offered her protection. As in 'A Poison Tree', we see the woman retreating further into the world of deceit, putting up self-delusory 'defences' with which, in the final stanza of the poem, she repulses her would-be guardian and retreats into the harsh and thorny world of the old maid (compare this with 'My Pretty Rose Tree' and 'The Lily'). The pulsing regularity of the iambic tetrameter emphasises the hard, bristling exterior the woman has adopted.

'The Tiger'

Many interpretations have been put forward for this poem, but it seems to operate most effectively in the realm of uncertainty — to pursue one single train of thought would be to limit its rich possibilities. The following is a brief outline of some useful ideas and approaches:

- **Context** provides a useful way in to the poem. In stanza five Blake poses the question 'Did he who made the lamb make thee?', specifically guiding the reader to draw comparisons with 'The Lamb', and pointing towards the central role of contraries in the collection as a whole. Indications can be found throughout the poem of how the tiger and the lamb differ, and it might be fruitful to ask what these differences suggest about the nature of God, their creator.
- **Blake's mythology** (see pp. 76–79) provides further illumination. The figure of Orc is frequently associated with fire, one of the key images of the poem. He is always presented as being energetic and creative. We might infer from this that the tiger, far from being a bearer of destruction, is a symbol of creative power and beauty — a figure of vitality, liberty and desire.
- **Classical mythology** also offers a useful insight. According to myth, Prometheus stole the fire of the gods for the sake of man, thus literally 'seiz[ing] the fire'. He is also associated with mythical stories of creation which provides another connection with the poem.

■ **Revolution** is another key concept. Refer to pp. 17–18 for an exploration of this issue.

The poem's iambic rhythm is forceful and pulsing, and is used to reinforce various aspects of the poem — it reflects the tiger's relentless pacing, the beating of its heart, and the rhythmic blows of the hammer against the metal. Alliteration and repetition are used to create tension. The tiger's orange and black colouring is created by the contrasting 'burning bright' and 'night', the dangerous connotations of which suggest a more fearsome hunter than the placid beast of Blake's illustration. The reference to the 'night' is fitting, as darkness offers ideal conditions for tigers to stalk their prey.

Blake thus establishes the tiger's dangerous nature straight away, but his uncertainty of how it came into being is signalled by his use of rhetorical questions throughout the poem. In contrast to 'The Lamb', there are no simple answers. We are told that the tiger is the creation of an 'immortal hand or eye', and the power of its creator is stressed throughout. However, if it was made by the divine hand that created the lamb (a question posed explicitly in stanza five), Blake might be revealing God's harsh and unpalatable side. God would therefore embody contraries of tenderness and power. This mixture of beauty and terror is another of Blake's contraries, and in the final stanza the word 'dare' tellingly replaces 'could' in the final line. This reflects the way in which our view of the creator has changed through the poem.

Blake employs the extended metaphor of a blacksmith to describe the tiger's creation. The harshness of the blacksmith imagery — a process dependent on fire — suits the harshness of both creature and creator, whether it be God or Satan. This account of the creative process could not be more different from the piper's description in 'Introduction' (I). Words such as 'twist', 'beat', 'dread' and 'deadly terrors' all suggest danger — it is almost as if the animal is fighting with its maker in the very act of creation. The materials from which it is made are unbendingly resistant, as suggested by the use of the 'hammer', the 'chain' and the 'anvil'. The assonance of 'twist the sinews' creates an aural impression of the creative act, and the menacingly pulsing rhythm that accompanies the beating of the heart gives a sense of urgency. Some critics have sought to relate this directly to the revolutionary spirit of Blake's time, seeing in the use of the word 'terrors' a specific reference to the Terror, a period of bloody retribution following the French Revolution. But despite the violence of the creative process, Blake does not allow his reader to lose sight of the tiger's beauty. The act of creation might require the power of the blacksmith's 'shoulder', but also demands his 'art', in the sense of both craftsmanship and aesthetics.

This poem does not present an unquestioning, ideal view of the relationship between the spiritual and the earthly. The creator's nature is called into question as

Blake forces the reader to compare the creators of the tiger and of the lamb and to consider how they can be reconciled (see Isaiah 11:6–9).

'My Pretty Rose Tree'

Blake's original manuscript places this poem on the same page as two others, namely 'Ah! Sunflower' and 'The Lily', an unusual occurrence in the *Songs*. 'My Pretty Rose Tree' is the subject of the major illustration on the page — it depicts a female figure carelessly leaning against the roots of the rose tree, which presumably represents her. At her feet, cross-legged, sits a despairing male figure, his head buried in his arms. A flock of birds is seen in the distance, possibly representing the departing hopes of the young man.

The poem should be compared with the other flower poems that follow, but also with 'The Angel', in which the female persona arms herself 'With ten thousand shields and spears' to protect herself from the lover/angel, an image comparable to the thorns of 'My Pretty Rose Tree'. The 'thorns' also pre-empt similar thorns in 'The Lily' and the briars of 'The Garden of Love'. In all these poems the thorns appear as a mechanism of defence against a perceived sexual threat. 'The Angel' and 'My Pretty Rose Tree' can be seen as exploring the same event.

The first line of 'My Pretty Rose Tree' makes it clear that the male is subject to temptation, recalling the biblical tale of Adam and Eve. The temptation is symbolised by a flower of unsurpassed beauty. Unlike Adam, however, this male remains faithful to his rose tree in the face of his trial. His loyalty and dedication are evident in the opening of stanza two, where his attention to the rose tree is emphasised. The reader should be alert, however, to the warning inherent in the phrase 'by day and by night'; it echoes 'The Angel', in which the female persona 'wept both night and day', and 'A Poison Tree', in which the narrator tends his destructive passions, represented again by a tree, so that 'it grew both day and night'. As the connotations of the phrase hinted, the female is unreceptive and will not accept the devotion she is offered, imagining his infidelity and jealously keeping her beauty to herself.

'Ah! Sunflower'

The poem opens with an atmosphere of wistfulness and melancholy. The 'Ah!' is a sympathetic sigh for the condition of the sunflower, and gives an impression of its sad existence. It is 'weary of time' and mechanically 'countest the steps of the sun'. The last two lines of the first stanza describe the flower's hopeless search for the 'sweet golden clime' and its desired rest. These are, after all, literal impossibilities for a flower bound to the earth by its roots. On the other hand, even when it is melancholy the sunflower has aspirations (note that the word 'aspire' appears in line seven) and still hopes to achieve its desire.

As in 'The Angel' and 'My Pretty Rose Tree', in the second stanza Blake paints a picture of unfulfilled desire. The sunflower's yearning for the sun it can never reach (it is rooted to the ground) is a powerful metaphor for unrequited love. The youth who has 'pined away' and the image of the 'virgin shrouded in snow' suggest a deathly, enforced chastity. The latter image also contrasts with the brightness of the sunflower. The place of disappointment and sadness where these characters reside could be the 'golden clime' the sunflower desires.

Indeed, the place where the youth and the virgin live may actually be a place of hope. The words 'arise' and 'aspire' suggest resurrection. But if ultimate happiness and fulfilment are possibilities within the poem, they cannot be achieved in this lifetime — happiness lies beyond the grave. The final line of the poem, therefore, may be taken as a sign that the sunflower is yearning for death because this is the only way it can be fulfilled.

'The Lily'

This could be seen as an uncomplicated nature poem celebrating the beauty of the lily. Such a simplistic reading, however, is not satisfactory given that 'The Lily' is third in a sequence of flower poems about love. The first half of the poem, dealing with the more 'experienced' world of the rose and the sheep, employs the iamb, while the second section, looking at the 'innocent' world of the lily, uses a combination of iambic and anapaestic feet. This provides a rhythmic contrast between the two sections of the poem, reinforcing the differences between their attitudes to love.

The poem begins by recalling 'My Pretty Rose Tree', in that the rose's thorns give protection from the dangers of love and relationships. Extending the image further, Blake points out how sheep — which elsewhere symbolise purity — use their horns to defend themselves. The lily, a flower traditionally associated with purity and virginity, does not have any such means of defence. This may be a sign of its vulnerability in love and its openness to abuse. However, it is clear from the third and fourth lines of the poem that this is not necessarily a negative state of affairs — indeed, the lack of any protective mechanisms leaves the lily free to 'love in delight'. The thorn and the horn are perhaps blights on the perfection of the rose and the sheep. Lilies are also associated with funerals; the stillness of the second half of the poem, which contrasts with the activity of the first half ('puts forth'), perhaps suggests death.

'The Garden of Love'

It is interesting to compare this poem with 'The Echoing Green', which is about childhood freedom and the innocent love between the old and the young. Both poems use a combination of iambic and anapaestic feet but to different effect. 'The Echoing Green' has a light and tripping double measure, but 'The Garden of Love' adopts the heavier trimeter, suiting the irony of the poem and the harshness of its content.

The opening line is misleading, because the phrase 'Garden of Love' has joyful connotations. However, Blake's poems are rarely as simple as they seem. The presence of the chapel (conventionally a positive image) is ambiguous. Its position in the centre of the green suggests its dominance, and it acts as the antithesis of the childhood 'play' depicted in 'The Echoing Green' and 'Nurse's Song' (I).

Indeed, Blake hated organised religion, and the poem explores some of the restrictions he saw and detested in the church (see pp. 19–20 and pp. 29–30). The chapel is not therefore the welcoming and open place that we might expect, but is imposing and forbidding. The gates are shut to prevent approach (like the spears, thorns and horns of the preceding poems) and the chapel announces itself with the prohibition 'Thou shalt not'. The emphasis is on restriction and the curtailment of (innocent) freedom.

Turning to the garden, the speaker finds that the Eden-like paradise of 'The Echoing Green' has gone. Blake illustrates this by the lack of flowers — instead of containing the blooming beauty of life, the land is filled with graves, symbolic of the death of innocence, but also, perhaps, the graves of those who previously played on the green.

Blake saw organised religion as being profoundly at odds with the spirit of freedom and life. The disturbing image of the 'priests in black gowns…walking their rounds' makes them seem more like policemen of morality than priests of Christ. Blake emphasises his dislike of the priests by connecting the positive and the negative with internal rhymes in the final two lines of the poem ('gowns' and 'rounds', 'briars' and 'desires'). This has a deadening effect on the stanza's rhythm, and sits uneasily in the poem, neatly representing the restrictive effect of the priests. It is clear that 'joy' and 'desires' have no place in the priests' perception of life.

'The Little Vagabond'

The relationship between parents and children is a central concern of the *Songs*, and 'The Little Vagabond' begins with an appeal to the speaker's mother. This reinforces its links with the 'Chimney-Sweeper' poems. The first of these includes only a father, the second deals with both the father and the mother, and this poem deals with the mother alone. This completes the possible combinations of parent/child relationships, all of which seem to fail. The presence of the mother also recalls 'The Little Black Boy', 'A Cradle Song', 'Infant Joy' and 'A Dream'.

The opening line focuses directly on organised religion. As in 'The Garden of Love', Blake is critical; the cold church compares unfavourably with the warm ale-house, an ironic contrast that Blake uses throughout the poem. Despite conventionally being a place of sin and moral laxity, the ale-house is 'healthy and pleasant and warm', characteristics lacking in the church. The church, Blake suggests, has much to learn from the conviviality and companionship of the ale-house with its literal and figurative warmth. The boy's reluctance to remain in church with his mother does not indicate a heathenish lack of religious belief, but rather a culpable lack of warmth and compassion on the part of the religious establishment. The boy would 'sing' and 'pray' if only the church would welcome him.

According to the boy, the church needs 'pleasant fire our souls to regale'. Fire is a significant image for Blake, and in his poetry it is associated with creativity, energy and life. This is embodied in the figure of Orc (see p. 78), the spirit of energy, who Blake often depicts with or in fire. True spirituality and true religion, for Blake, cannot be divorced from the fire and creative energy of life — since God led the Israelites through the desert in a pillar of fire (recounted in the book of Exodus) and the Holy Spirit descended at Pentecost in tongues of fire (see Acts of the Apostles). Fire is also a central image in the creation of 'The Tiger'.

Blake's attack on the church continues through the poem. The suggestion that the parson would do well to drink makes the point that the church is detached from the pleasures of living, the needs of common people and the rituals of daily life.

The second half of the third stanza recalls 'The Schoolboy' (I). Blake again presents an oppressive teacher, 'modest dame Lurch'. Education is reduced to the punishments of 'fasting' and 'birch'; the children are 'bandy', a sign of rickets. The very name 'Lurch' suggests that the children have been abandoned, or 'left in the lurch' by their teacher; like the parents of 'The Chimney-Sweeper' (E), she 'is always at church', hypocritically ignorant of (or deliberately ignoring) the needs of the children in her care.

The final stanza recalls the parable of the prodigal son (see Luke 15:11–32), in which the wasteful and errant child is joyfully taken in when he returns home, emphasising the joyous and welcoming side of God's nature. Note the build up of internal feminine rhymes ('quarrel', 'Devil', 'barrel' and 'apparel') in the final two lines which give the vagabond's argument a sense of conclusiveness.

'London'

Along with 'The Tiger', this is probably the best known of the poems from the *Songs*. As a lifelong Londoner (see pp. 15–16), Blake was familiar with the city and its life, and this provides the backdrop to much of his work. Although this is a dark poem, the illustration that accompanies it seems to suggest more hopeful possibilities: an old man, led by the hand by a young boy, leaves a dark street to enter an apparently bright building. Below, on the right-hand side, is a picture of a child keeping warm by a blazing fire, which symbolises life and energy. However, these images can also be interpreted more darkly; the old man, perhaps representing wisdom, is being led by the child, a symbol of youthful inexperience, while the child at the fire may be a street child abandoned in the cold city. The poem employs a regular iambic tetrameter, sometimes in a truncated form. This may be taken to indicate the drudgery and psychological imprisonment that seems to be the common lot within the city.

It quickly becomes apparent that the poem is set in a world of uncertainty and ambiguity. An immediate ambiguity arises with the word 'chartered'. A charter is a document which has a number of possible meanings, some suggesting freedom (a bill of rights) and some suggesting limitation (a contract or a map). The interpretation of the word depends on our understanding of the rest of the poem. As the poem progresses, we need to identify the various connotations of privilege, freedom and possession that the word implies and to consider the ways in which Blake creates an ironic interplay between them.

In the opening stanza Blake draws the reader's attention to the ubiquitous frailty and sadness of the people of the city. 'Weakness' is embodied by the old man in the illustration accompanying the poem, who could be seen as a symbol for the city itself. Note the pun on the word 'mark', meaning first to observe and then a blemish or a sign.

The second and third stanzas move on to describe the city's soundscape: crying, shouting, sighs of death, the clinking of imaginary chains and prohibitions are heard everywhere. These sounds and emotions are not restricted to a few of the inhabitants of the city, but are the norm, as the repeated use of the word 'every' makes clear. The 'mind-forg'd manacles' are also common to everyone. They could have been created by the workings of the human mind and imposed on fellow human beings, just as 'The Chimney-Sweeper' (E) is made to suffer by the decision of his parents, 'The Little Black Boy' suffers through bigotry, 'The Little Boy Lost' (I) suffers through his misleading father and the children of 'Holy Thursday' (I) suffer through the supposedly charitable ministrations of the 'wise guardians of the poor'.

The presence of the chimney-sweeper in line nine recalls 'The Chimney-Sweeper' poems, placing the individual boys we have seen so far in the context of the city, where the 'black'ning church' and the 'midnight streets' add to the impression of urban decay and violence. The brutal reality of death, illustrated in the fate of 'the hapless soldier', is present, as is the threat of revolution in the blood on the palace — an image that would have been laden for Blake's contemporaries with echoes of the horrific excesses of the French Revolution.

The chimney-sweeper and the soldier are joined in stanza four by the 'youthful harlot' and the 'new-born infant' as victims of the city. The young woman is the dominant figure of the entire poem (she is heard the 'most'), and she resembles the prostitute riding the beast in Revelation 17, an embodiment of blasphemy and disease. Her plight is pathetic because, like the chimney-sweeper and the newborn infant, she is young but hopeless — she is a victim of the city and the society that uses her 'services'. She may wreck marriages (as is suggested by the final line) and carry diseases, but she is also a young woman forced to earn her living by selling her body. Her 'curse' echoes around the streets of the city, and might be taken to mean foul language or disease, but she could also be lamenting her great misfortune. Her voice blots out the cries of the 'innocent' babe, although the reader may well feel that she is scarcely more than an innocent babe herself.

'The Human Abstract'

This poem is the companion to 'The Divine Image' (I) and continues the exploration of human imprisonment from 'London'. 'A Poison Tree', which also uses the conceit of a tree (linked to the biblical Tree of Knowledge), provides further comparisons. One of the meanings of 'abstract' is summary, in which case the poem consists of a depressing definition of what it is to be human. The illustration accompanying the poem depicts a man tied down by ropes at the base of a tree. If the reader takes this man to be the 'He' of the poem and the tree to be the Tree of Knowledge, the image would suggest that the man is enslaved to the source of 'experience' or original sin, the cause of mankind's fall.

Like 'The Divine Image' (I), this poem begins with a consideration of mercy, pity, peace and love. Here, however, these qualities are modified by the impure and unfair world in which they exist. Pity and mercy do not arise from altruism, but from human neglect. Similarly, in stanza two, peace and love develop from the rather less praiseworthy contexts of 'mutual fear' and 'selfish[ness]'. Far from leading to goodness, as we would expect, they result in 'Cruelty' and imprisonment. This suggests a world of inverted morality, in which good and bad are inextricably entwined, and the human spirit is marred by deception and self-interest.

The image of the tree appears in the third stanza. Instead of leading to good fruits, 'holy fears' and 'Humility' result in a tree which casts 'the dismal shade/Of Mystery'. Instead of being liberated, the man finds himself further entrapped in the 'shade' of his own mind. The tree is symbolic of the dark and evil nature of mankind. This is emphasised by the parasitic 'caterpillar and fly' which feed off the man's dark and hidden desires.

As well as being central to the fall of mankind, trees appear frequently throughout the Bible. Although the fruit of this tree is 'the fruit of Deceit', it is superficially attractive, as it is in 'A Poison Tree'. The tree's true nature is suggested, however, through the presence of the raven, a bird frequently associated with death, and which disturbingly lurks 'In its thickest shade'. Blake equates this tree with the destructive influence of sin, suggesting that the tree is found within 'the human brain'. This, along with the similar points made in 'A Poison Tree', casts light on the image of the 'mind-forg'd manacles' of 'London'; it is evident that much of the suffering faced by humanity is caused directly by other humans following laws and rules instead of instincts and desires.

'Infant Sorrow'

'Infant Sorrow' is the contrary poem to 'Infant Joy' (I), and can be compared with 'The Little Black Boy', too. Blake's illustration develops that for 'Infant Joy',

suggesting that there is not just a contrasting, but also a sequential relationship between the two poems. If the reader takes the images of buds in 'Infant Joy' to be representations of the womb, then the illustration of mother and child accompanying this poem can be seen as the next step. It is interesting that while in 'Infant Joy' both mother and baby are given a voice, in this poem the baby alone speaks.

The poem explores the connections between childhood, 'innocence' and 'experience'. It begins on an ambiguous note, because the first line is open to two widely differing interpretations, each of which affect the reading of the whole poem. The groans of the mother may be caused by the pain of childbirth, and the tears of the father may express his happiness at the safe delivery of the child. If this is the case, Blake seems to be suggesting the presence, even from birth, of 'experience' (or original sin), because the child's reaction is incompatible with the love and affection demonstrated by its parents. Alternatively, the verbs 'groaned' and 'wept' might be taken to indicate the parents' sadness and distress at the birth of their child, in which case the child's behaviour might be a more understandable response.

In either case, the world is not inviting and pleasant, but 'dangerous'. The active verb 'I leapt', in place of the conventional and passive 'I was born', is startling, and indicates that the child is already a fully functioning individual, capable of making choices. The sense in which the child is 'Helpless' is therefore called into question — does this indicate that the child cannot fend for itself, or that it will not receive help? The word 'piping' recalls 'Introduction' (I), and in doing so demonstrates how far we have moved from the innocent joy the piper envisaged. Similarly, the phrase 'Like a fiend hid in a cloud' recalls 'The Little Black Boy'; here, however, the 'cloud' of the earthly body does not withdraw to reveal a 'white' soul; instead, it conceals a 'fiend', a shocking image to apply to a newborn baby.

Stanza two moves the reader still further from the conventional depiction of a baby. This child appears active and recalcitrant, 'struggling' and 'striving' against the restraints imposed upon it by its father and the swaddling bands. As the word 'bound' emphasises, these restraints are not seen as a form of protection, but as imprisonment. Blake seems to be suggesting (as in the 'mind-forg'd manacles' of 'London', and the literal enchainment of Earth in 'Earth's Answer') that imprisonment and sinful behaviour are innate; although newborn, the child understands this, as is shown by the 'weary' and deeply disconcerting resignation of the final lines.

'A Poison Tree'

The first stanza outlines what happens when anger is expressed or concealed, and stresses the importance of openness and honesty. The regular, rhyming form gives a deceptively simple, childlike feel to the stanza. The word 'wrath', and the exploration of man's relationship with his enemies, suggests the wrath of God, perhaps demanding that we compare the teachings of both the Old and New Testaments on jealousy and forgiveness.

As in 'The Human Abstract', Blake employs an extended metaphor of a tree. Springing from the word 'grow', this metaphor develops throughout the second and third stanzas. The 'fears' and 'tears' (which might be produced by anger, frustration or sadness) provide the perfect conditions for the tree to grow. These are accompanied by hypocrisy (the 'smiles' of line seven, which illustrate the dark pleasures of evil and which the 'tears' reveal must be mirthless) and 'soft deceitful wiles'. Note the reappearance of deceit, also a key component of 'The Human Abstract', and the subtle but highly effective juxtaposition of the words 'soft' and 'deceitful', suggesting the comfort and pleasure the man derives from his deceit. When the tree bears a fruit in stanza three, it is clearly evil, and the consummate expression of the poisonous effect of nurturing anger. It can also be seen as a lure, designed to provoke a further 'attack' from the enemy.

The events of the last stanza, which occur under the cover of darkness, have both spiritual and symbolic significance. The act of revenge alone is a dark act, but the fact that the avenger is 'glad' moves us into the deepest recesses of the human psyche. The reappearance of the word 'pole' is significant, too, as it recalls 'Introduction' (E) and 'Earth's Answer'. In those poems, the 'pole' is 'starry', representing heaven, for which humanity strives. Here, in contrast, the fact that the act is committed under cover of night suggests that the foe is seeking to hide from God, adding to the pervading sense of evil and deceit Blake creates.

'A Little Boy Lost'

In contrast to the 'Little Boy' poems in the *Songs of Innocence*, in this poem there is no hope of salvation, and no subsequent poem in which the little boy is 'found'. He faces his punishment alone and unsupported.

The poem opens with the little boy reflecting on how he sees himself. This can be interpreted in a number of ways:

- The focus on the self could be perceived as self-love, which continues the idea of 'selfish loves' from 'The Human Abstract'.
- Blake may be implying that humans can conceive of nothing greater than themselves because of the limitations of the human condition.
- If, as Blake suggests in 'The Divine Image', God is in every human, it would indeed be impossible for a human to conceive of something 'greater than itself'.

Whatever his meaning, this heretical view brings the boy into conflict with the teachings of established religion. His simile of the bird is taken as a sign of flippant ingratitude and disrespect towards his father — though notably not by his father himself, who (later joined by the mother) remains a marginal and powerless figure throughout the poem. Far from being disrespectful, the image is a touching expression of dependence and devotion. Like Cordelia in Shakespeare's *King Lear*, the boy damns himself through the honesty of his response.

Stanza three shows the child as the victim of cruel authority ('he seized his hair'), which seems to be out of control ('trembling zeal'). His plight is worsened by the tacit approval of the onlookers. Note the irony in the phrase 'priestly care', which continues into the following stanza as the boy is denounced as a 'fiend'. Despite claiming to preach the divine mystery, the priest's view is actually limited by the very 'reason' he attributes to the boy; he is unable to see for himself what the boy has already summarised in the two opening stanzas. In calling the boy a fiend (a word which harks back to 'Infant Sorrow'), the priest betrays himself to be just the kind of unthinking and inhuman judge he accuses the boy of being.

On the strength of the priest's views, however, and in spite of the tears of both himself and his parents, the boy is condemned to be sacrificed. The final stanza intimates that he is the latest in a long succession of those wrongly immolated as a result of the ill-informed perceptions of the religious authorities. The image of imprisonment (the 'iron chain') recalls 'the mind-forg'd manacles' of 'London' and the chained figure of Earth in the first two poems of the *Songs of Experience*. This emphasises the extent to which humans are limited and seek to limit each other.

The final line of the poem poses a rhetorical question, to which the reader is presumably meant to answer a horrified 'yes', especially in the light of poems such as 'The Chimney-Sweeper' (I and E), 'Holy Thursday' (I and E), 'The Little Vagabond' and 'The Garden of Love'.

'A Little Girl Lost'

In this poem which addresses the reader directly, Blake makes his indignation clear from the opening. The poem is an 'indignant page' through which Blake directly addresses his readers, the 'Children of the future age'. He envisages a future in which attitudes towards the fulfilment of sexual love will have changed, and the form of this first stanza, which is different from all the others in the poem, indicates its function as a prophetic introduction or prelude to the tale of Ona, her lover and her father.

The second stanza invokes 'the age of gold', a time of untroubled innocence representing Eden before the Fall of man. Unlike the frozen world of 'Earth's Answer' (which uses the same form and metre), this is a place of 'sunny beams' and is 'Free from winter's cold'. It is also a place of perfection ('Youth and maiden bright', 'holy light'), where nudity is not a source of shame, which is again redolent of the Garden of Eden. In stanza three the abstract youth and maiden become a specific 'youthful pair', Ona (whose name means grace, favoured by God) and her lover. Unlike 'Earth's Answer', where darkness reigns and the world is barren, the atmosphere is of lightness and life. The removal of 'the curtains of the night' suggests the coming of enlightenment, using a theatrical image to prepare us for the drama that follows.

Blake emphasises the innocence of the young people; 'On the grass they play' makes them appear childlike. This 'play' is the 'kisses sweet' of line 20, and it is really foreplay, taking place away from the restrictive eyes of the parents and other inter-fering adults. Blake implies that the parents would be incapable of seeing the innocence of their love and its expression. Note his use of the word 'fear'; Ona's loss of fear, leading to the sexual consummation of stanza five, is presented as a positive step, and by extension the sexual taboos and limited perceptions of her parents and of society appear to be an unwelcome and unjustifiable constraint.

The use of the adjective 'white' to describe Ona's father indicates his age, and perhaps links him to the hoary-headed and restrictive figure of Urizen (see pp. 78–79). It is revealing that Blake continues to refer to Ona as the 'maiden bright', as she appeared in line seven. Her innocence seems to be intact, as if her sexual act does not necessarily equate with 'sin'. Her father, however, clearly does not see it this way. Unlike the father in the parable of the prodigal son, a tale this poem inverts, this father is not a welcoming and joyful figure. Instead, like the priest of the preceding poem, he sits in judgement on his daughter. His 'loving look' — words laden with painful irony — only inspires terror in his daughter, and the reader wonders what kind of love can include such characteristics. Ona is instantly removed from her position of 'innocence' to a position of 'experience' or guilt. Her transformation is completed in the final stanza of the poem, in which the formerly anonymous 'maiden bright' becomes 'Ona! pale and weak'. It is significant that only at this point do we learn her name, as if it is another restrictive label or a badge of shame.

The father's selfishness is revealed by his focusing solely on himself. This is reminiscent of Earth's accusation in 'Earth's Answer' that God is the 'Selfish father of men', a parallel which is completed in the final line of the poem where it is 'the blossoms of [the father's] hoary hair' that are shaken, not those of his daughter, who has been 'deflowered', and has come to resemble Earth's frozen and bound state.

'To Tirzah'

The first stanza introduces the contrary states of imprisonment and freedom, or mortality and immortality. Lines one and two outline the inevitable fate of mortal man, which is death. The phrase 'consumèd with the earth' alludes to God's words to Adam after the Fall — 'for dust you are and to dust you will return' (Genesis 3:19) — making it evident that this is the universal lot of mankind. Line three then suggests that resurrection (or freedom from constraint) can only occur through the death of the earthly body. Blake seems to be indicating that the 'imprisonment' of the earthly condition that Tirzah torments men with is a false perception, hence the direct challenge he makes to her in line four, which is repeated at the end of the poem. This recalls Paul's first letter to the Corinthians (1:15), in which he challenges the power of death as a direct result of Christ's resurrection — this is alluded to specifically in the final stanza.

Stanza two continues in the same challenging vein. Its allusions to the Fall of man emphasise the limitations of the earthly body; the references include the sudden

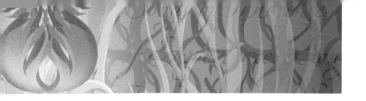

development of sexual consciousness in Adam and Eve and the punishment of man to undertake hard labour to survive (Genesis 3:17).

The third stanza presents Tirzah as a cruel parental figure, which connects her with many of the other parents and parent figures in the *Songs*, including the parents of 'The Chimney-Sweeper' (E), and even God himself in 'Introduction' (E) and 'Earth's Answer'. Using language that echoes 'The Tiger', Tirzah 'mould[s]' the heart of her creation. The binding up of the senses of the earthly body, a curious act of *un*creation, reduces humans to the mere 'senseless clay' of the fourth stanza — a state of living death perilously close to the dead earth of the opening stanza — if they fail to see beyond the perceived bounds of 'mortal life'.

It is only by seeing through the confines of mortality, which is made possible through the death and resurrection of Jesus, that humans can cope with the limitations and psychological repressions of this life and can shake off the fetters with which Tirzah seeks to enchain them. The earthly body is transient. Death is not the end, but only a form of sleep prior to resurrection. For a biblical exposition of these concepts, refer to 1 Corinthians 15:35ff.

For more on Tirzah, see p. 78.

'A Divine Image'

The characteristics of cruelty, jealousy, terror and secrecy are by now familiar after their exposition in poems such as 'The Human Abstract', 'A Poison Tree' and 'A Little Girl Lost' (E). Similarly, the imagery of the forge used in stanza two recalls 'The Tiger', illustrating the destructiveness and the harshness of human nature.

The poem is even more condemnatory in its view of humanity than 'The Human Abstract', and is an alternative partner poem to 'The Divine Image'. At the end of the *Songs*, the reader is left with a clinical and dark view of humanity in which the presence of the divine is hard to trace.

Blake's mythological world

Throughout his life, Blake lived in a visionary world of angels, spirits and the heavenly realms. It is therefore not surprising that his poems often seem prophetic, and that many of his later works operate on a grand scale. As his poetic world developed, he devised a set of mythological and highly symbolic characters to people it. In the years surrounding the publication of the combined *Songs of Innocence and of Experience* (1793), Blake published a sequence of prophetic books, all of which employ these mythological characters. Reading passages from works such as *America, a Prophecy, Europe, a Prophecy, The Book of Los, The Book of Ahania* and *The Visions of the Daughters of Albion* will further your understanding of Blake's complex theological, political and sociological views.

These mythological characters do not actually appear in the *Songs*, with the exception of 'To Tirzah', which was probably added after their initial publication, but it is helpful to be aware of the existence of this pantheon. Blake uses his characters to encapsulate particular concepts, many of which apply directly to the *Songs*. These are outlined below.

Albion

Derived from the Latin word 'albus', which means white and refers specifically to the white cliffs of Dover, Albion is a poetic name for England. Occasionally Albion appears as an energetic and happy figure, but more often, as in *Milton* and *Jerusalem*, he appears either sleeping, suffering or in despair. The character of Albion can be compared to the personified Earth in 'Earth's Answer'.

Bromion

Meaning 'roar' or 'inarticulate sound' in Greek, Bromion is a figure of unbridled physical desire. In *The Visions of the Daughters of Albion* he rapes Oothoon and thus seems to represent violent sexual passion. Issues of sexual desire inform a number of the *Songs*, such as 'The Little Girl' poems, 'London' and 'A Poison Tree'.

Enitharmon

The wife of Los, Enitharmon represents the failings of earthly religion. She is led astray by the concepts of chastity and vengeance, which occur frequently in the *Songs*; you should refer to 'The Little Girl' poems, 'London' and 'A Poison Tree'.

Los

Los represents the imagination and the creative faculties, and is a counterpart to Urizen (see below). Los is a craftsman, often appearing as a blacksmith. The imagery of a blacksmith at work is used in 'The Tiger', and as such the poem may be interpreted as a celebration of creative energy. Indeed, Blake often equates Los with Christ because of his love and forgiveness.

Luvah

Peter Ackroyd describes Luvah as 'the principle of sexual energy', and as such he is comparable with Bromion. His association with energy, however, which was valued by Blake, makes him a more positive figure. In 'A Little Girl Lost' (E), Ona and her lover seem to represent this positive, sexual energy.

Oothoon

Oothoon symbolises innocent sexuality and the political freedom of North America. She can be compared with the figure of Lyca from the *Songs*, as well as other characters innocently exploring their sexuality.

Orc

In *America, a Prophecy*, Orc is described as a 'Lover of Wild Rebellion, and transgressor of God's Law'. He is a figure of revolution, inspired by a love of freedom and is often associated with fire. He contrasts with Urizen, a bearded old man, because he is presented as a vigorous, energetic and lustful youth. The *Songs* raise issues of lust and suggest the possibility of revolution, within both the individual and society. Concepts of freedom and constraint lie at the heart of the *Songs*, and they are key to understanding Orc's nature.

Theotormon

With a name combining the Greek word 'theo' (god) and 'torment', Theotormon is a tortured figure. He represents mankind's suffering under the restrictions of conventional morality. The *Songs* contain many such figures, no doubt inspired by Blake's profound dislike of organised religion, for example in 'The Chimney-Sweeper' (E), 'Holy Thursday' (E) and 'The Garden of Love'.

Tirzah

Tirzah appears in the Bible as both one of the five daughters of Zelopehad (Numbers 27:1–2) and as a city in Israel, the capital of the Ten Tribes (1 Kings 15:33–34). In the former story, Tirzah and her sisters are central to the establishment of a binding legal principle of inheritance, and in the latter story the city is the seat of an evil king who sets himself in opposition to Jerusalem, the city of God. Both ideas are central to Blake's mythological figure, whose deadly binding of humanity sets her in direct opposition to God. Robert Gleckner (1959) sees her as a figure of consummate experience seeking to bind humanity, and whose song's 'opposite and contrary cannot be found in any song of innocence but in the concept of innocence as a whole'.

Urizen

The name Urizen may derive from a corruption of 'your reason', implying an external (perhaps imposed) wisdom. Alternatively, it could come from the Greek verb 'horizein', which means 'to limit'. Both interpretations suggest important aspects of Urizen's character. Always appearing as an elderly figure, often using measuring instruments, he is the God of the Old Testament; a creative but also a restraining force. Peter Ackroyd describes him as 'tyrant, priest and lawgiver'. He contrasts with Orc and Luvah. In the *Songs* his likeness can be seen in poems such as 'The Chimney-Sweeper' (E), where freedom and justice are denied to the innocent boy, and 'The Little Vagabond', where happiness is forbidden. The figure of God in 'Introduction' (E) and 'Earth's Answer', and the father in 'A Little Girl Lost' (E), also bear similarities to the figure of Urizen.

The emergence of Orc in *America,*
a Prophecy

Urizen beneath the tree of mystery
writing secrets of wisdom

Musical interpretations of the *Songs*

Music is an important idea in the *Songs of Innocence and of Experience*. The *Songs of Innocence* begin with a piper, and the *Songs of Experience* are introduced by a bard. Blake is thought to have made up melodies for some of the *Songs*; Edward Garrard Marsh, responding to a letter written in 1802 by Blake's friend William Hayley, refers to an occasion when Blake had evidently sung some of the *Songs*:

> I long to hear Mr Blake's devotional air, though (I fear) I should have been very awkward in the attempt to give notes to his music. His ingenuity will however (I doubt not) discover some method of preserving his compositions upon paper, though he is not well versed in bars and crotchets.

It seems that Blake never did manage to preserve his own music for the *Songs*, yet many subsequent musicians have produced a range of interpretations of his works. The lack of any interpretations prior to the modern day is interesting — Parry's

famous 1917 music for 'Jerusalem' is the earliest. This suggests the extent to which Blake's vision was ahead of his time. The moral and spiritual complexities of his poems seem to have appealed more widely to the modern world than to any other age. If possible, you should listen to some of the recordings detailed below and consider how they interpret the poems.

Classical

Ralph Vaughan Williams and Benjamin Britten are among the classical composers who were inspired to set Blake's poems to music. Vaughan Williams composed *Ten Blake Songs for Voice and Oboe* (Andante, 1999); Britten wrote *Songs and Proverbs of William Blake* (Decca, 1965), and the 'Elegy' section of his *Serenade* (Decca, 1963) includes a setting of 'The Sick Rose'. Other composers include:

- Hubert Parry — his setting for the hymn 'Jerusalem' is from *Milton* (Phillips, 1996)
- Lucien Posman — *Ten Songs of Experience* (Cyprès, 2002)
- Ned Rorem — 'The Sick Rose' and 'Spring' (Naxos, 2002)
- John Tavener — 'The Lamb' and 'The Tiger' from *Song for Athene* (Naxos, 2000)

Modern

In 1971, Bob Dylan and the beat poet Allen Ginsberg collaborated on settings for 'Nurse's Song', 'A Dream' and 'The Tiger', which, although unreleased, were performed on US television. More recently, the jazz-punk artist Jah Wobble has released *The Inspiration of William Blake* (Hertz Records, 2000). His music for the *Songs* contrasts strongly with the traditional, classical settings. Further rock recordings are listed below:

- Greg Brown — *Songs of Innocence and of Experience* (Red House Records, 1986)
- Finn Coren — *The Blake Project* (Bard Records, 1997)
- Fester and Massa — *MoM (Man on the Margin)* (Studio Records, 1998)
- Greg Forbes — *Songs of Innocence and of Experience* (Echoing Green Music, 1998)

Poetic metre

Analysing why a poet has chosen a particular metre can shed light on the reading of a poem. However, as with the use of any technical terminology, you should make sure that your discussion of poetic metre is linked closely to the discussion of the poem and its content.

The metre, or 'measure', of a poem is the pattern formed by its sequence of syllables. The ways in which metrical form is applied varies from country to country;

in the French and Japanese traditions, for example, it is the number of syllables alone, without consideration of stressed and unstressed syllables, that is measured (syllabic metre), while the Roman and Greek traditions emphasised the importance of metrical feet (a unit made up of a particular combination of long and short syllables), which appeared in fixed numbers within lines of verse (quantitative metre). In English verse, the approach is slightly different to either of these. English poetic metre is based on the difference between stressed and unstressed syllables and their combination. Lines are defined by the number of stressed syllables they contain and may also include further regularity in terms of the number of syllables they contain in total.

The analysis of a poetic line is known as **scansion**, and always comes in two parts. First, the metrical foot is identified, and then the number of feet in the line.

Metrical feet

The main types of metrical feet used in English verse are identified below, where / is used to indicate a stressed syllable and ~ denotes an unstressed syllable:

iambic	~ /		**dactylic**	/ ~ ~
trochaic	/ ~		**spondaic**	/ /
anapaestic	~ ~ /		**pyrrhic**	~ ~

You should always look closely at the use the poet makes of stress patterns within each line, because this can frequently highlight certain words or characteristics essential to a fuller understanding of the poem. The following example from 'London' is written in the **iambic** form:

~ / ~ / ~ / ~ /
I wander through each chartered street,

~ / ~ / ~ / ~ /
Near where the chartered Thames doth flow,

Because these lines use only one type of metrical foot, they are **regular**. 'The Shepherd' includes **anapaestic** lines, which give a gentle rhythm:

~ ~ / ~ ~ / ~ ~ /
For he hears the lamb's innocent call,

~ ~ / ~ ~ / ~ ~ /
And he hears the ewe's tender reply.

Again, the lines are written in one kind of foot and are regular. However, the regular line can be modified by omitting one syllable (usually the first). When this happens, the line is known as a **catalectic** or **truncated** line. 'The Tiger', which uses the **iambic** foot, provides an example:

/ ~ / ~ / ~ /
Tiger, tiger, burning bright,

/ ~ / ~ / ~ /
In the forests of the night:

Here the initial unstressed syllable has been omitted, which gives the poem a forceful, aggressive rhythm.

It is also possible for poets to use a combination of metrical feet within a single, complex line to achieve a variety of rhythmical and emphatic effects. The opening stanza of 'Nurse's Song' (I) provides a good example of this:

~ ~ / ~ ~ / ~ ~ / ~ ~ /
When the voices of children are heard on the green

~ / ~ ~ / ~ ~ /
And laughing is heard on the hill,

~ / ~ ~ / ~ / ~ /
My heart is at rest within my breast

~ / ~ ~ / ~ /
And everything else is still.

This is a combination of **anapaestic** and **iambic** feet. Concluding the stanza with an iambic foot gives it the sense of closure the poem describes.

Metre

Having identified the metrical foot (or feet) a line of poetry uses, the next step is to work out how many feet the line includes. The types of feet are as follows:

dimeter	two feet
trimeter	three feet
tetrameter	four feet
pentameter	five feet
hexameter	six feet
heptameter	seven feet

A line of verse is classified according to the type and the number of feet. Thus, a poem employing four regular iambic feet is written in **iambic tetrameter**.

Types of love

All of the poems in the *Songs of Innocence and of Experience* are about love or the lack of it. The table below categorises the poems according to the kind(s) of love with which they deal.

	Empathy/love for mankind	Divine love	Parent/child love	Romantic/ sexual love	Love of nature
'Introduction' (I)			✓		
'A Dream'			✓		
'The Little Girl Lost' (I)			✓	✓	✓
'The Little Girl Found' (I)			✓	✓	✓
'The Blossom'			✓	✓	
'The Lamb'			✓		
'The Shepherd'			✓		
'On Another's Sorrow'	✓	✓	✓		
'Spring'					✓
'The Schoolboy'	✓		✓		✓
'Laughing Song'	✓				✓
'The Little Black Boy'	✓	✓	✓		
'The Voice of the Ancient Bard'		✓			
'The Echoing Green'	✓				✓
'Nurse's Song' (I)	✓				✓
'Holy Thursday' (I)	✓	✓			
'The Divine Image' (I)	✓	✓			
'The Chimney-Sweeper' (I)	✓	✓	✓		
'A Cradle Song'		✓	✓		
'The Little Boy Lost' (I)			✓		
'The Little Boy Found' (I)		✓	✓		
'Night'		✓			
'Introduction' (E)			✓	✓	
'Earth's Answer'		✓			✓
'The Clod and the Pebble'	✓				
'Holy Thursday' (E)	✓				✓
'The Chimney-Sweeper' (E)	✓	✓	✓		

	Empathy/love for mankind	Divine love	Parent/child love	Romantic/sexual love	Love of nature
'Nurse's Song' (E)	✓				
'The Sick Rose'				✓	✓
'The Fly'		✓			✓
'The Angel'	✓				✓
'The Tiger'	✓	✓			✓
'My Pretty Rose Tree'	✓			✓	✓
'Ah! Sunflower'	✓			✓	✓
'The Lily'	✓			✓	✓
'The Garden of Love'	✓	✓			
'The Little Vagabond'	✓	✓	✓		
'London'	✓		✓	✓	
'The Human Abstract'	✓	✓			
'Infant Sorrow'	✓		✓		
'A Poison Tree'	✓	✓			
'A Little Boy Lost' (E)	✓	✓	✓		
'A Little Girl Lost' (E)	✓	✓	✓	✓	
'To Tirzah'	✓				
'A Divine Image' (E)	✓				

Animal imagery

Blake frequently uses animal imagery in the *Songs of Innocence and of Experience*. The following table identifies the majority of the animals to which Blake refers and suggests their symbolic significance.

Animal	Poem(s)	Symbolism
Ant	'A Dream'	vulnerability; hard work
Beasts of prey	'The Little Girl Lost'; 'The Little Girl Found'; 'Night'	threat
Beetle	'A Dream'	guidance
Caterpillar	'The Human Abstract'	destruction
Fly	'The Fly'; 'The Human Abstract'	decay; disease; satanicalness; vulnerability
Glow-worm	'A Dream'	guidance; light; hope
Grasshopper	'Laughing Song'	happiness
Lamb	'Introduction' (I); 'The Lamb'; 'The Shepherd'; 'Spring'; 'The Little Black Boy'; 'The Chimney-Sweeper' (I); 'Night'; 'The Tiger'	innocence; sacrifice; vulnerability; Christ; children; Christian believers
Leopard	'The Little Girl Lost' (I); 'The Little Girl Found' (I)	threat
Lion(ess)	'The Little Girl Lost' (I); 'The Little Girl Found' (I); 'Night'	danger; protection; royalty
Raven	'The Human Abstract'	death
Robin	'The Blossom'	innocence
Sheep	'The Shepherd'; 'Nurse's Song' (I); 'Night'; 'The Lily'	innocence; vulnerability; followers

Animal	Poem(s)	Symbolism
Skylark	'The Echoing Green'	innocence
Sparrow	'The Blossom'	innocence
Thrush	'The Echoing Green'	innocence
Tiger	'The Little Girl Lost' (I); 'The Little Girl Found' (I); 'Night'; 'The Tiger'	threat; revolution; creative energy; God
(Wild) birds	'On Another's Sorrow'; 'The Schoolboy'; 'The Echoing Green'; 'Night'; 'The Little Vagabond'; 'A Little Boy Lost'	threatened innocence; imprisonment; freedom
Wolves	'Night'	threat
Worm	'The Sick Rose'	destruction; death; disease; male sexuality; Satan
Wren	'On Another's Sorrow'	innocence; vulnerability

Literary terms

The terms and concepts below have been selected for the relevance to writing about the poems in *Songs of Innocence and of Experience*. It will aid argument and expression if you become familiar with them in your essays.

allegory	extended metaphor conveying moral meaning
alliteration	use of repeated consonant letter sounds for effect
allusion	reference, either direct or indirect, to other texts
anapaest	a metrical foot of three syllables arranged ~ ~ /
anthropomorphism	attributing human characteristics to an inanimate object
antithesis	contrast of ideas expressed by parallelism
assonance	repetition of vowel sound in words in close proximity
black humour	makes fun of something serious
caesura	deliberate break in a line of verse, usually signified by punctuation
characterisation	the ways in which an author creates and develops a character
contextuality	historical, cultural, social, economic and political background of a text
couplet	pair of consecutive rhyming lines
dactyl	metrical foot of three syllables arranged / ~ ~
didactic	adjective applied to a work of literature setting out to promote or teach a particular religious, political or philosophical point of view
dimeter	line composed of two metrical feet
enjamb(e)ment	run-on line of verse, usually to reflect meaning
end-stopped	pause created by punctuation at the end of a line of verse
epigraph	inscription at the head of a chapter or book
genre	type or form of writing

hexameter	line composed of six metrical feet
iamb	metrical foot of two syllables arranged ˜ /
imagery	descriptive or figurative language; often appeals to a variety of the senses — touch, taste, smell, sight, sound
internal rhyme	rhyme occurring within a line of poetry
irony	language intended to mean the opposite of the words actually employed; an amusing or cruel reversal of a situation
juxtaposition	placing ideas, characters or events side by side for (often ironic) contrast or to create other types of literary connection
metonymy	substituting an attribute for the thing itself, e.g. 'crown' for monarchy
metre	the dominant pattern formed by sequences of syllables
metrical foot	unit of stressed and/or unstressed syllables
myth	story about supernatural beings
omniscient narrator	narrator who has God-like powers to see all events, actions, motivations and thoughts
parable	story used to illuminate a moral lesson
pathetic fallacy	use of the weather or the landscape to reflect events, moods etc.
pathos	sad situation, evoking pity in the reader
pentameter	line composed of five metrical feet
personification	human embodiment of abstraction or object, using capital letter or she/he
plurality	possibility of multiple meanings of text
pyrrhic	metrical foot of two syllables arranged ˜ ˜
quatrain	set of four lines of verse
register	level of formality in expression
sestet	set of six lines of verse
spondee	metrical foot of two syllables arranged / /
stereotype	typical characteristics of a category of person, often used for mockery
symbolism	use of characters, actions, objects to represent higher, more abstract concepts
synecdoche	form of metaphor in which a part (often a body part) is used to represent the whole
tetrameter	line composed of four metrical feet
trimeter	line composed of three metrical feet
trochee	metrical foot of two syllables arranged / ˜
unreliable narrator	narrator the reader does not feel able to trust (due to age, naivety, self-delusion, tendency to lie, political reasons etc.)

Questions & Answers

Essay planning

This section gives two essay titles followed by suggested plans. The plans are much longer than would be realistic for an examination essay and the points identified would need to be illustrated carefully with well-chosen examples and quotations from the poems.

1 **Blake lived in an era of considerable political upheaval and social change. How does his use of language and form in the *Songs of Innocence and of Experience* reflect this?**

Possible plan

Blake's poetry in the *Songs* consistently engages with the world in which he lived, and reflects his views about the political and social changes occurring around him.

Political and social issues

- political revolutions abroad (especially the upheavals in France and America) and the fear of revolution at home
- industrial revolution in Britain, which led to a vast shift in working practices and living conditions as enormous urban expansion began
- Britain's rapid expansion as an imperial power
- the phenomenal growth of London and the huge divide between the rich and the poor within the city, many poor inhabitants living and working in appalling conditions
- religious authority and restriction and its legitimacy

Key poems and discussion points

- 'The Tiger' — can be seen as a representation of the revolutionary spirit and its power and unpredictability; identify Blake's links with revolutionary politics, including his connections to Romanticism and his trial for sedition; also discuss his use of fire imagery — a traditional symbol of revolution — in many of the poems.
- 'London', 'The Tiger', 'The Chimney-Sweeper' (I and E) — Blake represents London as a huge and dirty city, blackened by the smoke of industry; 'The Tiger' employs industrial imagery to convey the creation of the tiger; boys such as Tom Dacre and his nameless counterpart from the *Songs of Experience* were the product of the new, urban industrial society, and Blake champions the cause of their liberty.
- 'The Little Black Boy' — there are suggestions in this poem that Blake engages with issues of empire, challenging the morality of slavery and the slave trade; his appeal to common humanity can be seen as progressive.
- 'London', 'Holy Thursday' (E) — Blake reveals the evils of the dark and threatening city; he shows the victims of urban existence, highlighting the poverty in which

many are forced to languish and the cold charity on which they are forced to depend.

- 'The Garden of Love', 'A Little Boy Lost' (E), 'A Little Girl Lost' (E) — Blake explores the power of organised religion; he evidently despises this authority and its restrictions, which he sees as contrary to the nature of God; Blake identifies the social impact of organised religion; outline Blake's unconventional religious views and links to Swedenborg's ideas.

Language and form

- wide variety of rhythmical forms employed for effect
- repeated imagery of fire, imprisonment, tears and fears to convey meaning
- repeated use of innocent victims
- close structural and verbal links between poems
- device of pairing poems
- meaning and significance of contraries

2 In 'The Chimney-Sweeper' (I), Blake presents his reader with the situation of Tom Dacre. Comment on the detail of his situation, focusing particularly on his dream and its impact on the reader. How does this poem relate to its partner, 'The Chimney-Sweeper' (E)?

Possible plan

The speaker's circumstances

- he has been sold to a chimney sweep by his father
- he is an orphan
- he is virtually a slave
- he lives and works in appalling conditions

Tom's dream

- Tom is presented as a sacrificial lamb — connections with Christ, suggesting holiness and innocence
- dream seems to offer a vision of hope
- use of coffins emphasises the dangerous nature of the boys' work
- boys' conditions reflect badly on the parents who have sold them
- dream seems to offer escape and liberty from the death and slavery of the chimney-sweepers' work
- rural images and cleanliness contrast to urban reality of filth
- angel suggests God's desire to free the boys
- nakedness and whiteness of boys in the dream contrasts with the spiritual blackness of their lives and their physical blackness from the soot
- final stanza sees the boys return to work — the vision has offered hope

Compare and contrast the poems

- the second poem is much more pessimistic and offers no hope, unlike the first poem which looks at the state of 'innocence'
- role of organised religion more overtly questioned in the *Songs of Experience* poem to convey hypocrisy and lack of true charity
- both poems address the idea of 'duty' — in his innocence Tom is unaware of the full implications of duty and who should be showing duty to whom (the final line is ironic); experience makes clear where duty has not been fulfilled by the parents
- both poems consider the difference between appearance and reality — through the dream in the former poem and through the parents' and the boy's behaviour in the latter
- repeated use of 'weep weep' ties the poems verbally; they also share a common metrical form to emphasise their connections
- snow of the *Songs of Experience* poem suggests greater harshness and coldness, which is echoed in the tone of the poem
- the actual conditions of these boys is the same, but their perceptions are very different — perhaps it is in perception that the difference between 'innocence' and 'experience' lies

Examination essay titles

The titles that follow can be used for planning practice, full essay writing practice or both. They may be used as a support for class discussion or collaborative work, or on an individual basis for timed or extended writing. You should be aware of the need in all responses to refer closely to the text (even in closed book exams), supporting your arguments and comments with succinct and relevant evidence. Where appropriate, you may also choose to incorporate relevant critical material as a basis for your argument and response.

Whole text questions

1 Blake was an advocate of social responsibility and justice. How do the *Songs of Innocence and of Experience* reflect this?

2 Blake lived the majority of his life in London. Discuss his portrayal of the urban environment in the *Songs of Innocence and of Experience*.

3 Comment in detail on Blake's presentation of children and childhood in the *Songs of Innocence and of Experience*.

4 Discuss Blake's presentation of sexual experience in the *Songs of Innocence and of Experience*.

5 Comment in depth on the attitude towards organised religion that Blake expresses in the *Songs of Innocence and of Experience*.

Prescribed passage-based questions

Examiners advise that a substantial portion (up to 60%) of responses to passage-based questions should refer to the rest of the work being studied. For Blake, you are likely to be asked to concentrate on one poem. Focus on the poem selected, but refer to other relevant poems too for comparison and contrast. It is essential to demonstrate how the poem operates within the *Songs* as a whole. Establish the context of the poem and then explore how it links to the rest of the *Songs* in terms of theme, structure and technique. Where a specified aspect of the poem, such as Blake's use of language or imagery is identified, ensure that this is a central element in your response.

1 Read 'The Echoing Green' and then answer *all* of the following questions:
  - Comment on the location and atmosphere of the poem.
  - How does Blake use language and form to present these to the reader?
  - Discuss Blake's presentation of location and atmosphere elsewhere in the *Songs of Innocence and of Experience*.

2 Read 'The Clod and the Pebble' and then answer *all* of the following questions:
  - Discuss the views of love Blake conveys in the poem.
  - How does Blake use contrast and irony in the poem?
  - Choose two or three other poems that deal with love, and explore their relationship with 'The Clod and the Pebble'.

3 Read 'The Sick Rose' and then answer *all* of the following questions:
  - What possible meanings does the poem convey?
  - How does Blake use language and imagery to make these meanings?
  - Comment on how Blake uses flower imagery elsewhere in the *Songs of Innocence and of Experience*.

4 Read 'London' and then answer *all* of the following questions:
  - What impression do you gain of the city?
  - Explore Blake's presentation of the characters in the poem.
  - Comment on one or two other poems in which Blake explores human nature.

5 Read 'Nurse's Song' (I) and then answer *all* of the following questions:
  - What impression do you gain of the Nurse?
  - How do the form and language of the poem contribute to this impression?
  - With reference to one or two other poems, comment on the relationship between adults and children in the *Songs of Innocence and of Experience*.

Self-selected passage-based essays

When a task gives the option of selecting your own passages for specific reference, it is essential to select carefully. Failure to do so can lead to digression and even irrelevance. In the case of Blake, make sure that you clearly identify the poems you choose and that they enable you to address the issues identified in the question

specifically and in detail. Remember, the poems you know and/or like best are not necessarily the most appropriate choices.

1 Blake's ideas were significantly influenced by the writings of Rousseau and Swedenborg. Choose one or two poems where such an influence is evident, and comment more widely on the presence of such ideas in the *Songs of Innocence and of Experience.*

2 How does Blake convey his thoughts and feelings about the treatment of power and wealth in the England of his day? In your answer, *either* make detailed use of one or two of his poems *or* range widely across the *Songs.*

3 Animal imagery is frequently used in the *Songs of Innocence and of Experience.* Using examples from several poems, explore the effects Blake creates by using this type of imagery.

4 In the *Songs* Blake deals with a number of types of love. Explore at least two of these types, *either* making detailed use of one or two of his poems *or* ranging widely across the *Songs.*

5 The expressed intention of the *Songs* is to show the 'Two Contrary States of the Human Soul'. *Either* explore this assertion by comparing a pair of poems of your choice *or* range widely across the *Songs.*

Sample essays

Below are two sample essays of different types. Both have been assessed as falling within the top band. You can judge them against the Assessment Objectives for this text for your exam board and decide on the mark you think each deserves and why.

Sample essay 1

Read 'The Little Black Boy' and then answer *all* of the following questions:
- Comment on Blake's presentation of the concepts of 'black' and 'white' in the poem.
- Explore the relationship between the black boy and the white boy.
- Referring to a range of other poems, explore Blake's presentation of the under-privileged in the *Songs.*

'Black' and 'white' are key concepts in this poem. On one level the colours are used as a straightforward designation of skin colour, a feature which points out the physical differences between the two boys in the poem. However, Blake's intentions and techniques must be examined more deeply. Black and white are polar opposites, and Blake's choice of these colours might be a manifestation of the contraries that play such an important role in the *Songs.* On the volume's title page, Blake states that he intends to explore the 'Contrary States of the Human Soul', and the reader is therefore encouraged to see in Blake's use

of the black boy and the white boy two contrary versions of humanity. It would be a mistake, however, to see this division as a straightforward — or black-and-white — proposition: such a reading would be far too simplistic.

Underlying the images of 'black' and 'white' is a wealth of traditional assumptions. In spiritual terms, black is usually associated with darkness and evil, while white is associated with light and goodness. In the first stanza, however, Blake undermines these ideas, showing that judging either boy on the basis of his skin colour is inappropriate and wrong:

> And I am black, but oh! my soul is white.
> White as an angel is the English child;
> But I am black as if bereaved of light.

The simple equation of white with goodness and black with evil was prevalent in Blake's society, a time when the slave trade was yet to be abolished. In challenging the conventional notions about colour, Blake is setting himself against his society's acceptance of slavery.

As the poem progresses, Blake redefines the respective values of black and white. The black boy appears to be the spiritual superior of the white boy, who remains unable to 'love' him yet. The black boy's skin is an advantage in the 'southern wild', and Blake equates the heat of the African sun with the 'heat' of the divine presence of God, who gave the black boy his skin. The black boy demonstrates genuine altruism and goodness in seeking to protect the white boy from the fierce rays of the sun. Although we are only given the perspective of one child, it is possible to trace a deepening relationship between the two boys — and it is notable that the black boy makes all the positive gestures. The black boy envisages a time when their physical differences are put behind them ('When I from black and he from white cloud free') and they can meet on the common ground of spiritual equality. When this happens, they will:

> ...lean in joy upon our father's knee,
> And then I'll stand and stroke his silver hair
> And be like him, and he will then love me.

Blake's use of pronouns is significant here — the distinction between 'him' and 'me' ceases to exist, becoming subsumed in the common 'our'. Sadly, however, the black boy seems to recognise that such a reconciliation will never happen in the boys' lifetime — the image of them becoming 'free' of their 'cloud[s]' suggests death. The distinctions between black and white remain firmly in the reader's mind throughout the poem as a continuing barrier to the achievement of the ideal union, whereby these two 'lambs' can stand together before their creator.

There are many significant comparisons that can be made between this poem and others in the *Songs*, in which Blake frequently considers the plight of the underprivileged. First and foremost, Blake aims to challenge stereotypes and to attack the accepted relationships between those in positions of power and authority and those helplessly exposed to it. Just as the conventional view of the relationship between the black boy and the white

boy in pre-abolition England is undermined through challenging the connotations of 'black' and 'white', so are the reader's views of the 'wise guardians of the poor' challenged in the 'Holy Thursday' poems, where their charity and treatment of the helpless children in their care are exposed as rank hypocrisy. Blake is keen to encourage his readers to question what may constitute good and evil.

In a similar way, Blake repeatedly forces the reader to evaluate the role of organised religion in society and exposes its failure to support its most vulnerable members in poems such as 'The Little Vagabond', 'The Garden of Love' and 'The Chimney-Sweeper' (I and E). He powerfully presents the ways in which the religious establishment at best fails to prevent suffering and at worst seems actively to encourage the maltreatment of underprivileged children. Blake perceived this as profoundly contrary to his vision of God; passivity for Blake was an expression of evil, and as such the passivity of the church in the face of social depri-vation and other social evils was a sign of its separation from the truth of God, who he thought of as an active force for good. The little black boy can be compared directly with other victims of social prejudice and inactivity, such as the chimney-sweepers (who are also 'black' boys, covered as they are in the soot from the chimneys). Blake describes the chimney-sweeper of the *Songs of Experience* as 'A little black thing among the snow', and Tom Dacre's white hair is spoiled by the soot.

'London' provides another interesting comparison. The streets of the city are filled with the victims of social injustice. Everywhere the poet turns he is faced with 'Marks of weakness, marks of woe' and signs of mental and physical imprisonment similar to the restraints faced by the little black boy. The underprivileged are everywhere — the chimney-sweeper, the 'hapless soldier', the new-born infant (who represents the hopelessness of the future), and the 'youthful harlot'. Although they symbolise the darkness of the city, these characters also illustrate the profound pity Blake feels for those who are forced to suffer as a result of the ignorance and carelessness of those around them.

Sample essay 2

What influence did Blake's interest in the Old and New Testaments of the Bible have on his *Songs*?

Blake was a profoundly religious man, brought up in the dissenting tradition, so it is not surprising that he looked to the Bible for poetic inspiration. This influence is evident throughout the *Songs*. Sometimes this manifests itself in direct reference to biblical passages, at other times biblical stories, characters and concepts are alluded to, and on other occasions Blake borrows the style and tone of the Bible. The literary heritage of the Bible is never far below the surface of the *Songs* and impinges on almost every element of Blake's poetry. His use of biblical material, however, is often idiosyncratic, as were his own beliefs, which were heavily influenced by the writings of Swedenborg, the Swedish theologian.

The division of the Bible into two sections — the Old Testament and the New Testament — is, in itself, significant. Throughout his life, Blake was fascinated by the concept of contraries and their impact on humanity. The biblical narrative is divided into contrasting halves: the first half focuses on God the father, whilst the second half focuses on Christ (God the son); in the Old Testament God often appears as a distant figure, whereas Christ (God in human form) appears closer to and more intimate with mankind; the God of the Old Testament is often vengeful, but Christ represents forgiveness. These ideas can be found in the *Songs*, in which Blake explores the contrary states of God (as in 'The Lamb' and 'The Tiger') and the differing aspects of humanity's relationship with God.

The opening two poems of the *Songs of Experience* are a good example of Blake's use of biblical material, as Blake invokes the story of Adam and Eve. Earth, a symbol of the fallen creation, is sought by God in a cold and cheerless environment far from the perfection of the Garden of Eden. The pain in their relationship is all too clear, as God calls longingly and almost despairingly for Earth to return to him, and Earth herself, resentful of the punishment inflicted on her, rebels still further. Blake uses the biblical story, with its aftermath of restriction and punishment, to establish the fundamental division between God and humanity in the world of 'experience'.

He uses the story of Adam and Eve again to great effect in two further poems in the *Songs of Experience*: 'A Poison Tree' and 'The Human Abstract'. In these poems Blake employs the image of the tree as a symbol of human failing and disobedience. According to Genesis, Adam and Eve disobey God in eating fruit from the Tree of the Knowledge of Good and Evil, and Blake draws on the tree's powerful symbolism. In 'The Human Abstract', a poem which summarises human nature, a tree is used to represent the human mind, a place where caterpillars and flies (both symbols of destructiveness) abide alongside the raven (a symbol of death). In invoking the image of the tree Blake suggests that these un-desirable characteristics are inherent within the human psyche as a direct consequence of sin and the Fall of man. The image of the tree is developed further in 'A Poison Tree'. Here it symbolises the growing conflict between two humans — or possibly even between God and his creation. The tree eventually grows a poisonous fruit which, when plucked and eaten, leads to death.

As well as using Old Testament imagery, Blake reflects on religious issues, such as the nature of God's relationship with his creation, for example in 'The Divine Image'. Here Blake pursues the idea, following the teachings of Swedenborg, that God resides in all humans and that all humans are, therefore, divine. The perfect representation of the divine human is Christ, and in the *Songs* Blake makes use of many of the biblical symbols associated with him. The lion (a symbol of Christ in both the Old and New Testaments, particularly in the apocalyptic books) appears most notably as the regal lion in 'The Little Girl Lost' (I) and 'The Little Girl Found' (I). The lamb, another key biblical representation of Christ, is found in 'The Lamb', in which Blake explores the connections between the divine and humanity. It also appears to considerable effect as a contrast in 'The Tiger', and 'The Chimney-Sweeper' (I), where it symbolises Christ-like innocence and sacrifice. Blake draws on the image of Christ as the good shepherd on a number of occasions, too.

It is not only in specific biblical allusions that we see the influence of the Bible,

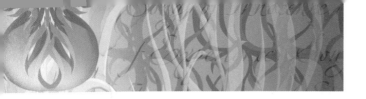

however. As a social observer, Blake was keenly aware of the importance of applying what he considered to be essential biblical principles to the world around him. Poems such as 'The Chimney-Sweeper' (I and E), 'Holy Thursday' (I and E), 'The Little Vagabond' and 'The Little Black Boy' demonstrate the consequences of human failure to apply the basic principles of love and true charity. Where these principles are not applied, we see the triumph of the human abstract over the divine image. The streets of 'London' are dangerous and dark places, devoid of true love and human fellowship. This pattern is repeated throughout the *Songs*, as 'selfish loves increase' ('The Human Abstract') at the expense of divine love. This contrast is perhaps most explicitly invoked in 'The Clod and the Pebble', a poem in which Blake overtly explores selfish and selfless love.

Finally, Blake's language is hugely influenced by that of the Bible. By incorporating words and phrases from scripture within the fabric of his writing, Blake maintains an integral link between his own words and the words of the Bible. This means that his work often takes on the tone of biblical text, whether in the simple language of Jesus' parables, the wisdom of the Proverbs or the prophetic books of the Old Testament, such as in 'The Voice of the Ancient Bard' or 'Introduction' (E). Biblical language is also found in the complex theological exposition of the New Testament letters of Paul (as in 'The Clod and the Pebble'), the epic narrative of the stories of Genesis, or the bizarre and visionary qualities of the apocalyptic books. The writings of the Old and New Testament, with their embodiment of contraries within unity, are the very backbone of the *Songs*.

Using the critics

The role of literary criticism and literary theory in the study of literature at both AS and A2 is central. Assessment Objective 4 requires students specifically to 'articulate independent opinions and judgements, informed by different interpretations of literary texts by different readers'.

While this does not necessarily mean that all such interpretations should be by established literary critics or propound particular theoretical readings, the implication that these should be covered as part of advanced study is clear, especially where incisive and detailed analysis is required. Furthermore, the emphasis placed on a range of readings makes the use of criticism essential to success.

The following is an extract from the AQA specification, developing some of the implications of Assessment Objective 4:

Candidates will be expected to show awareness of the following:
- that, as readers, we are influenced by our own experiences, actual or imagined, and that our cultural background has an effect on our interpretation; thus the interpretation of literary texts, or the determination of their significance, can depend on the interpretative stance taken by the reader

- that there might be significant differences in the way literary texts are understood in different periods, and by different individuals or social groups
- that texts do not reflect an external and objective reality; instead they embody attitudes and values
- that there are different ways of looking at texts, based on particular approaches and theories. Using these theories will require some understanding of critical concepts and terminology.
- that literary texts are frequently open-ended, so ambiguity and uncertainty are central to the reading of texts. Examination tasks will therefore expect candidates to take part in genuine critical enquiry rather than responding to tasks where the teacher/examiner already knows the 'right' answer.

You need to think carefully about how critical material should be used. The emphasis in examination specifications is placed firmly on a student's ability to recognise and evaluate the validity of interpretations from many viewpoints. Approaching a text from a single critical perspective, therefore, or prioritising one at the expense of others, is neither desirable nor helpful. Successful students apply and develop their critical thinking about the set text in the light of a variety of secondary critical texts.

It is essential, however, that you should not see the use of critical quotation as a virtue in its own right. Unthinking application of critical material is at best redundant and at worst prevents students from thinking for themselves. The key to successful application of literary criticism and literary theory is to use it as a basis for argument. There are three basic positions that can be adopted:

(1) To agree with a critical proposition and to use this to support an argument or part of an argument.

(2) To agree with qualifications with a proposition; identify clearly what the areas of agreement are, but go on to develop areas of disagreement, qualification, modification or extension of the ideas.

(3) To disagree with a proposition, explaining why.

All of these stances can be developed by going on to propose alternative critical or theoretical possibilities and evaluating the validity of one critical perspective over another in relation to the text or passage under consideration. To extend and enrich a response, the criticism used must be engaged with. Students need to identify clearly the issues raised by the critic, apply these in detail to the set text — which must always remain the primary focus of the response — and then evaluate by giving a personal judgement.

References and further study

Collected works

Butter, P. (ed.) (1996) *William Blake*, Everyman's Poetry, J. M. Dent.

Keynes, G. (ed.) (1966) *Blake: Complete Writings*, Oxford University Press. (This contains Blake's major poems, *Poetical Sketches*, Blake's annotations to Swedenborg and Reynolds, letters and other writings.)

Biographies

Ackroyd, P. (1995) *Blake*, Minerva.

Chesterton, G. K. (1978) *William Blake*, R. West.

Gardner, S. (1968) *Blake*, Evans Bros.

Gilchrist, A. (1863 and 1880) *The Life of William Blake*, Macmillan.

Larrissy, E. (1985) *William Blake*, Blackwell.

Criticism

Bentley, G. E. (ed.) (1969) *Blake Records*, Clarendon Press.

Bentley, G. E. (ed.) (1975) *William Blake: The Critical Heritage*, Routledge and Kegan Paul.

Botrall, M. (ed.) (1970) *Songs of Innocence and of Experience, a Casebook*, Macmillan.

Butler, M. (1981) *Romantics, Rebels and Reactionaries*, Oxford University Press.

Damon, S. (1988) *A Blake Dictionary: Ideas and Symbols of William Blake*, University Press of New England.

Dorfman, D. (1969) *Blake in the Nineteenth Century*, Yale University Press.

Ferber, M. (1985) *The Social Vision of William Blake*, Princeton University Press.

Frye, N. (ed.) (1966) *Blake: A Collection of Critical Essays*, Prentice-Hall.

Frye, N. (1972) *Fearful Symmetry*, Princeton University Press.

Gardner, S (1986) *Blake's Innocence and Experience Retraced*, Athlone Press.

Gillham, D. G. (1966) *Blake's Contrary States*, Cambridge University Press.

Gleckner, R. (1959) *The Piper and the Bard*, Wayne State University Press.

Lindsay, D. W. (1989) *Blake's Songs of Innocence and of Experience*, Humanities Press International.

Phillips, M. (ed.) (1978) *Interpreting Blake*, Cambridge University Press.

Raine, K. (1969) *Blake and Tradition*, Princeton University Press.